THE NAME
OF DEATH

THE NAME OF DEATH

KLESTER CAVALCANTI

Translated from the
Brazilian Portuguese by Nick Caistor

SEVEN STORIES PRESS
New York • Oakland • London

Seven Stories Press
140 Watt Street
New York, NY 10013
www.sevenstories.com

Library of Congress Cataloging-in-Publication Data

Names: Cavalcanti, Klester, author. | Caistor, Nick, translator.
Title: The name of death / by Klester Cavalcanti ; translated from the Brazilian
Portuguese by Nick Caistor.
Other titles: Nome da morte. English
Description: New York, NY : Seven Stories Press, 2018.
Identifiers: LCCN 2017056337 (print) | LCCN 2017061773 (ebook) | ISBN
9781609808297 (Ebook) | ISBN 9781609808280 (pbk.)
Subjects: LCSH: Santana, Jâulio, 1954- | Assassins--Brazil--Biography.
Classification: LCC F2538.5.S25 (ebook) | LCC F2538.5.S25 C3813 2018 (print)
  | DDC 364.152/4092 [B] --dc23
LC record available at https://lccn.loc.gov/2017056337

Book design by Jon Gilbert

Printed in the USA.

9 8 7 6 5 4 3 2 1

This book is dedicated to my parents, Déborah and Alcindo.

Also to my son, Diego.

ACKNOWLEDGMENTS

To my brother, Kaike Nanne, for his ever-present love and support. To my friends Alexandre Mansur, Janduari Simões, Roberto Sadovski, and Valdemir Cunha, for their constant encouragement. To Isabel Malzoni, for her patience and dedication.

CONTENTS

Author's Note

IT TOOK SEVEN YEARS of interviews before Júlio Santana authorized me to put his real name in this book. The first time we spoke, in March 1999, he agreed to tell me his story, but did not want to reveal his identity or to allow me—or anyone else—to photograph him. That's easily understood. The man I started to interview from that day on—at an average of once a month—is a professional killer who in thirty-five years of work has shot almost five hundred people. More precisely, 492 deaths, of which 487 were duly recorded in a notebook, with the date and place of the crime, how much he received for the "job," and most important of all, the names of those who contracted him, as well as those of the victims.

My first contact with this intriguing Brazilian citizen came about while I was working on a report about slave labor. At that time, in March 1999, I was *Veja* magazine's correspondent in Amazonia, a post I held for a little more than two years. For the report, the photographer Janduari Simões and I traveled to various towns in Pará state, looking for people who had been enslaved and for ranchers who kept slaves on their properties. During an operation by the Federal Police and the Ministry of Justice in the town of Tomé-Açu, one of the policemen said it was common in the region for the ranchers to hire gunmen to kill relatives—usually the children or brothers—of slave workers who had fled their estates, as a way of forcing the slaves to return to work. Seeing my interest in talking to one of these killers, a policeman taking part in the operation told me he knew a gunman and would speak to him to see if he could give me his phone number. To anyone who knows how the Brazilian police operate, unfortunately this friendly relationship between criminals and the police is nothing new. But I only really believed this federal policeman was going to put me in touch with the killer two days later, when he contacted me to say he had already talked to the gunman and that I could phone him the next day, at precisely two o'clock in the afternoon. The number he gave me was a public phone opposite a bakery in the town of Porto Franco, in Maranhão state. On that Thursday, March 18, 1999, in a conversation that lasted almost half an hour, I learned that the name of the man whose story I wanted to tell was Júlio Santana, and that he had committed his first murder at the age of seventeen, in 1971.

From our conversation and his tone of voice, Júlio did not seem to me either violent or aggressive. He spoke in a calm, unhurried way, with a strong northeastern Brazilian accent. What was clear from our first contact was that he was keen to tell his story. "If you like, I'll tell you everything," he said. "I've never told anyone these things." Before our conversation ended, we agreed to talk again five days later, at the same time. As soon as I hung up, I called the then executive editor of *Veja* in São Paulo, Laurentino Gomes, who had to approve my story ideas. He was enthusiastic about us doing the profile of a contract killer. But he said we could not publish such an outlandish, shocking story without at least giving the real name of the person involved. And if the killer agreed to pose for a photo, better still. Each time I talked to Júlio, I became increasingly fascinated by his story. But at the same time my hopes of him agreeing to us publishing his name and photo grew fainter and fainter. In the short term at least.

For the next seven years I continued my conversations with the man who killed close to five hundred people and never had any other profession. With every phone call our relationship became increasingly close. I felt as if he grew to trust me more and to tell his stories more sincerely and with greater emotion. Occasionally I would remind him of my wish to publish the story of his life—by now with the idea of making it into a book— but repeated that to do so it was absolutely necessary for him to authorize me to give his real name and a photograph. Júlio remained adamant. I was sure, though, that one day he would change his mind. This happened in January 2006. During one of our conversations, Júlio told me he had decided to abandon his life as a killer in order to live with his wife and two children in another state far away from Maranhão.

On hearing this, I managed to convince him that his greatest fear—that of being arrested if his name appeared in a book—no longer made any sense. Given that he was living in another state and leading a completely different life from the one he had led until now, the police would never find him. "But if you put my photo in the book, they'll get me," Júlio said. I explained that the photo was indispensable but that we could doctor it so that his face would be unrecognizable. And as a proof of the extreme trust he had in me, he finally agreed to let me to put his name and photograph in the book. This book.

Yet something important was still missing: to meet the killer in person. Up until then, all my conversations with Júlio Santana had been by telephone. I had no idea what he looked like, how he walked, how he sat, how he smiled. I did not know the house he lived in, or his wife and children. In order to get to know him and his universe, in April 2006 I traveled to Porto Franco, where Júlio and his family lived. I spent three days there with a calm, good-humored, home-loving man who was affectionate toward his wife and children and very religious. A man apparently nothing out of the ordinary. A very different profile from that of the killers that abound in literature and the cinema.

WITH THREE NOTEBOOKS stuffed with notes exclusively from my conversations with Júlio, I turned to another aspect of my work: to find other sources, both documents and people, who would confirm—or not—the stories told by the protagonist of this book. To do this I interviewed almost forty people—from policemen to gold prospectors who worked at Serra Pelada, and including relatives of people killed by Júlio. I also had access to police investigations and judicial files. It was a relief to discover that these sources, both people and documents, convincingly confirmed everything Júlio had told me, as well as providing me with detailed information about the cases referred to in this book.

One of the most surprising testimonies was that of the former parliamentarian and president of the Workers' Party,

José Genoino Neto. In his conversations with me, Júlio Santana had claimed he had taken part in the capture of José Genoino during the Guerrilla of Araguaia in April 1972. To test the truth of this story, I went to interview Genoino at his house in São Paulo. During our conversation I told Genoino that one of my sources (I did not reveal who it was) had claimed he had helped capture him in Araguaia. I recounted the story exactly as Júlio had told it to me, down to the smallest details such as the color of the dog that was in the hut where they captured the erstwhile guerrillero. When I finished, José Genoino confirmed everything. "There's no doubt that person was there," he told me. "You've just told me details I've never revealed to anyone." Genoino even remembered that in the group that caught him there was a boy who was much younger than the others. That boy was Júlio Santana, who at the time was only seventeen.

The story you are about to read describes the life of a man born in a village in the midst of the Amazon jungle who seemed destined to become a peaceable fisherman lost in the depths of the rainforest, like so many others in Amazonia. People abandoned by the authorities and government, in whose settlements even today there is no electricity, running water, sewers, schools, or health clinics. Where security is nonexistent, and where the police never set foot. A universe where nature is incredibly beautiful, filled with fascinating animals, centuries-old trees, and seemingly endless rivers. Out of this fabulous, inhospitable universe came Júlio Santana, a Brazilian who spent his life killing Brazilians. And anyone who thinks that these crimes were committed only in the depths of Amazonia is mistaken. In his thirty-five years as a contract killer, Júlio shot and killed people in many states, including São Paulo, Paraná, Bahia, and

Goiás. But he was always proud to declare that he never killed anyone out of hatred or for personal reasons. "I only kill when I'm paid to do so," he told me time and again. And despite having almost five hundred deaths to his name, Júlio Santana was only arrested once, in May 1987. He hopes never to go through that again.

The First Contract

FOR MORE THAN three hours, Júlio Santana had been spying on the fisherman Antônio Martins in the middle of the Amazon jungle, on the border between Maranhão and the north of Goiás (in what today is the state of Tocantins, created in October 1988). Despite the intense heat, Júlio felt strangely cold. His stomach was churning. Hidden among the age-old trees, some of them more than 130 feet tall, he kept the fisherman in the sights of his rifle. From the undergrowth, Júlio could see Antônio seated in his canoe, floating on a branch of the river Tocantins. He knew exactly what to do. "A single shot to his heart. End of story," he told himself. But for a boy just turned seventeen who had never before fired at a human being, it did not seem such a simple task.

At five feet nine and weighing 143 pounds, Júlio was skinny, his cheeks still smooth, with a long nose, thin lips, and black, thick, curly hair. His dark skin contrasted with his light brown eyes. That afternoon of August 7, 1971, he was trying to follow the instructions his uncle, the military policeman Cícero Santana, had given him the previous night: "Aim for his heart and imagine that you're shooting an animal, like when you're hunting." But shooting at a man made the boy feel strangely uneasy. It was not the same as killing pacas, peccaries, monkeys, or deer, as Júlio was accustomed to do in order to put food on the table at home. Disturbed by this unnerving situation, he sat on the ground, still damp from the night's rain. Placing the rifle between his knees, he leaned back against a Brazil nut tree and reflected on how he had got here.

IT HAD ALL BEGUN two days earlier. Around five in the afternoon, Júlio was returning from the jungle. After almost four hours' hunting, he was coming home with a young deer slung across his shoulders. Its flesh would feed the family for at least a week. The boy felt proud of himself. He had killed the deer with one well-aimed shot to the forehead. Júlio lived with his parents and two younger brothers: Jorge, aged forty-three, and his wife Marina, thirty-eight years old; Pedro, who was fourteen, and Paulo, aged eleven. The family lived in a wooden house in a riverbank community on the river Tocantins, in the municipality of Porto Franco, in the southwest of Maranhão state. In the early 1970s, the region was completely isolated and covered in virgin forest. Porto Franco had roughly 1,500 inhabitants— since then the number has risen to eighteen thousand. The family house had no internal partitions. The wood fire was on the left of the entrance. A raised plank on the floor separated the fire and the kitchen utensils—three pots, some cutlery, two large knives, and five glass cups—from a piece of furniture made by Seu Jorge which was sometimes used as a closet. No table or chairs. Electricity had not yet reached this far—even today, many communities in the region still have no access to it. There were five hammocks that were always slung, where the members of the family slept. Júlio also had an older brother, Joaquim, aged twenty-one, who had left his parents' home at eighteen and traveled to São Luis, the capital of Maranhão, where he thought he could find a better life. The family never had any further news of their firstborn.

BEFORE HE REACHED home after hunting, Júlio saw, tied to a tree trunk, the *voadeira* or aluminum motorized canoe belonging to his uncle Cícero. Aged thirty-one at that time, Cícero Santana had grown up in the same region. At fifteen, he had gone to Imperatriz, another town in Maranhão state, to try his luck. Then one day he turned up in Porto Franco in a uniform and told them he had joined the military police. The family was very proud of him. Cícero loved to hunt and fish, to explore the jungle. He was the one who taught Júlio to shoot. By the age of eleven, the boy could hit an animal on the far side of the river at a distance of a hundred yards. The many hours he and his uncle spent together roaming the forest, practicing shooting, hunting, fishing, and swimming in the muddy waters of the river Tocantins led to a close friendship everyone praised.

WHEN HE SAW his uncle's canoe, Júlio shifted the deer on his shoulders and quickened his pace. Cícero had not been to visit the family for two weeks. He usually spent a few days resting up at Júlio's house at least once a month. Before entering the house, Júlio dropped the deer carcass by the door, then ran proudly toward his uncle.

"Uncle, come and see the animal I shot. It's a young deer. I killed it with a bullet to the head, just like you taught me. Its meat must be delicious," said Júlio.

"Well done, kid," Cícero replied, smiling at his brother Jorge. "Let's see it," he said, putting his arm round his nephew.

That night a full moon lit up the forest, reflecting on the waters of the river and making it seem like dawn. During their supper—fried fish with rice and manioc meal—Cícero commented on the presence of soldiers from São Paulo, Brasilia, and Pará in the region between Porto Franco and Marabá in the southeast of Pará state. The small towns in the area were teeming with army personnel.

"They say they're searching for the communists hidden in the jungle round the river Araguaia and near here as well," said Cícero.

"There's no talk of anything else around these parts," said Júlio's father, but the boy didn't seem to be paying much attention to what they were discussing.

"The army says the communists want to destroy Brazil and that we can't let that happen. The army is calling on the people of the region to help them in this war."

"And how are the people supposed to help, Cícero?" Marina asked her brother-in-law.

"I have a friend who is the police chief in Xambioá [a town in the north of Tocantins state, on the banks of the river Araguaia]. He says the army needs people who know the forest in that region really well and can serve as guides in their operations in the jungle. They also need people who can shoot to help them in their hunt for communists," Cícero replied.

When he heard this, Júlio, who until then had shown no interest in their conversation, spoke up:

"I can shoot, and I know the jungle like the back of my hand. Will you take me with you to do that, Uncle?" asked the boy.

"Don't be silly, son. Do you think it's a joke?" snapped Dona Marina, scolding him.

AFTER SUPPER, seeking refuge from the intense heat, Cícero and Júlio went out for a ride in the canoe. It was just after seven in the evening. They went down a branch of the river Tocantins for twenty minutes, then landed the canoe on a beach some hundred yards long in the heart of the forest. Taking off their clothes, they entered the warm water. They could hear the din made by the creatures of the jungle: the cries of the toucans and macaws never stopped. They could even hear the growl of a puma. Accustomed to living in the Amazon, they knew they had no reason to worry about this wild beast. A puma would never enter the water to attack a person. Still less in the Amazon rainforest, where a predator of that size would have no difficulty finding food.

CÍCERO PICKED UP the bottle of cachaça he'd brought and offered it to Júlio. "Don't have too much, or you'll get drunk. I don't want your mother giving me a lesson again," said Cícero, who had already been told off several times by Dona Marina for giving his nephew alcohol. But Júlio really liked cachaça: he had learned to appreciate drink with his uncle from an early age. He never liked the taste of beer, but could not do without cachaça. The two of them stood in the water chatting for more than an hour, mostly about soccer, drink, and women. Cícero was the only member of the family whom Júlio had told that he was in love with Ritinha, a fourteen-year-old girl with dark hair, big eyes, and a plump mouth. She lived in a village an hour's canoe ride from his house. Their adolescent romance had begun two months earlier.

"She's beautiful, Uncle," said the boy.

"And does she have a beautiful body as well?"

"And how! Ritinha has got legs and an ass that drive me crazy."

"Have you done it already?"

"Done what, Uncle?"

"You know what, Julão," said Cícero, using the nickname "big Júlio" he'd given him because he was almost six feet tall. No one else called Júlio that.

"No, Uncle. We haven't done that yet," the boy replied with a wry smile. "But only because she wouldn't let me. I've already tried twice. She lets me touch her little breasts and her ass. But when I try to move my hand there, she pulls it away and says it's too soon."

"Great. Keep trying, and one of these days she'll open her legs."

Even today, Júlio remembers he did not like the way his uncle referred to the girl. Despite this, he thought it was funny and felt more confident that sooner or later he would lose his virginity with Ritinha. They were still in the water when his uncle suddenly said he felt cold.

"Are you sick, Uncle? It's hot as hell and you say you're cold!" said the boy.

"I think we've been in the water too long, Julão. Let's get out onto the sand."

So they climbed out of the water and returned to the beach. Even after drying himself on his shirt, Cícero kept complaining about the cold. He also said he had a headache: "I think bathing like that wasn't good for me. Let's go back to the house." When they got there, Cícero headed straight for his hammock. Seu Jorge and the other two boys—Pedro and Paulo—were already asleep. Dona Marina got up from the hammock where she was lying down beside her husband. The first thing she did was sniff her son's breath. She could not smell the cachaça, but knew Júlio and Cícero had been drinking. Both of them had been chewing ginger to disguise the smell of rum, and Dona Marina was well aware that there was only one reason for chewing ginger at night after a trip in a boat.

"You've disguised the stink of cachaça with ginger, haven't you? Do you think you can fool me?" she said. "At least you don't look drunk, like the last time," she said, addressing her son.

"I only had two swigs, Mom," said Júlio, who was always very respectful toward his parents.

"Okay. But it looks as if your uncle drank the rest of the bottle. He can't even stay on his feet."

"No, it's not that, Mom. He doesn't feel well. He says his head aches and he is cold."

Dona Marina went over to her brother-in-law, who was groaning and complaining of pains all over the body. She placed the palm of her right hand on his forehead, then ran it down his face and chest. He had a high fever.

"Where does it hurt, Cícero?" she asked.

"My whole body, Marina. My whole body," he replied.

Dona Marina covered her brother-in-law with her sheet and Júlio's. She put a piece of cloth soaked in cachaça on his forehead and declared: "It's malaria." What she said worried Cícero, but he didn't have the strength to get a word out. Dona Marina went back to her hammock and gave Júlio the responsibility of keeping an eye on his uncle. "If he gets worse, call me," she told him. The boy spent the rest of the night at Cicero's side. His uncle couldn't stop moaning. In the early hours, Júlio fell asleep seated on the wooden floor, leaning against his uncle's hammock.

By seven in the morning, the whole family was awake. Cícero was still in his hammock, complaining of a fever and an aching body. He said he felt nauseous. The family ate breakfast—bread, manioc, and fried fish, with coffee. Seu Jorge took a piece of bread and a cup of coffee to Cícero. He did not want to eat, but his brother forced him to. Cícero thought he must have caught malaria on one of his work trips into the depths of the rainforest. Now there was nothing to be done except wait for the symptoms to subside—even today, there is no cure for malaria. Dona Marina was dealing with the deer Júlio had hunted the day before. Seu Jorge had left to catch some fish for lunch. And Pedro and Paul had paddled their canoe to the community school: a wooden hut built in a village thirty minutes by boat from their house. The school taught up to fourth year, which Júlio had finished at fourteen. But with Cícero ill, he felt bound to stay at his side.

The two of them were alone in the house. It was then that Cícero began a conversation that was to torment Júlio ever afterward. Lying in a hammock next to his uncle, the boy was complaining about the intense morning heat when Cícero suddenly said:

"Julão, I need you to do something very serious and important for me. But you mustn't tell anyone. Not your parents nor your brothers. Not even Ritinha. No one."

"You can tell me, Uncle."

"This is very serious, Julão."

"Okay, Uncle, I heard you! You can tell me. You can trust me."

"I know I can. That's why you're the only person I can ask to do this."

"Why all this talk? Just tell me what it is, Uncle."

It was then that Cícero revealed something that surprised and frightened Júlio. In order to increase his earnings, his uncle combined his work as a military policeman with a very unusual activity. He was a hired killer. He had become part of the world of gunmen almost two years earlier. Júlio could hardly believe his ears. The uncle he loved so much was an assassin. Someone who killed others for money. He listened to Cícero's story with eyes wide open and his heart racing. He even thought his uncle must be joking or was delirious from his fever. But Cícero was talking so calmly and collectedly there was no room for doubt. It was all true. Even stranger was the way in which he had first got involved in this world.

HE TOLD JÚLIO that once, in October 1969, after he had been with the military police for two years, the battalion he belonged to caught three men suspected of executing four rural workers near the town of São Francisco do Brejão, in the west of Maranhão state. To Cícero's horror, one of the suspects was someone he knew, by the name of Arnaldo da Silva, a fruit seller in Imperatriz. When he asked Arnaldo why he had got mixed up in the business of murder, he told Cícero something that piqued his interest. The people who had hired them paid almost 1,000 cruzeiros—more than four times the minimum salary at the time, which was 225 cruzeiros, and more than twice what Cícero earned each month as a military policeman.

"You became a bandit for money, Uncle?" asked Júlio, dumbfounded.

"I'm not a bandit, my boy. If I didn't do it, others would take my place. In other words, the poor guy would die anyway. And this way at least I earn a bit more money."

"But you're a policeman! How can you be a policeman and a bandit at the same time?"

"I already told you, Júlio: I'm not a bandit. And it's thanks to those jobs I do as extra that I can get cash to buy certain things. What money did you think I used to buy my motorized canoe?"

Cícero struggled to say all this. His breathing was labored and slow. He went on to tell his nephew he had traveled from Imperatriz to Porto Franco—a distance of sixty miles—not just to see his brother and nephew again. He had been hired to kill a local fisherman. The victim was thirty-eight-year-old Antônio Martins, born in São Geraldo do Araguaia in the southeast of Pará state. With ancestors from the south of Brazil, the fisherman was known as Amarelo or "Yellow" because of his fair hair and light-colored skin. Antônio used to boast that he'd left São Geraldo do Araguaia after he stabbed to death the man his girlfriend was seeing. Everyone in the region knew this story about him. Even Júlio. This left him even more terrified.

"You're going to kill Amarelo, Uncle?" the boy gasped. He got up from his hammock.

"Sit down, Júlio. Why are you so upset?"

"Why am I so upset? Are you mad? You must be. You're going to kill Amarelo and you expect me to stay calm?" said Júlio, pacing up and down the room that was little more than sixty-five square feet.

"Keep your voice down, my boy. Do you want your mother to hear what we're saying?"

"Mom is outside on the riverbank, cleaning the deer. She can't hear us."

"If you carry on shouting like that, she's bound to hear. Sit down in the hammock and stay calm. I'm not going to kill Amarelo. I don't have the strength to get out of this hammock, still less to kill that bastard."

"That's good," said Júlio, sitting down once more. He was still settling into the moving hammock when Cícero said something that seemed to explode inside his head.

"You're the one who's going to kill Amarelo."

Júlio was left speechless. He remembers that his uncle went on talking, but he could not take in the words. He looked away toward the door at the rear of the house. The forest was glinting in the relentless sunshine. Accustomed to lengthy hunting trips in the jungle, his sharp eyes spotted a sloth clinging to a tree in the distance. The animal's gray fur stood out from all the surrounding greenery. Júlio suddenly felt envious of the peaceful life the sloth seemed to lead. He lifted his left leg out of the hammock, pushed against the wooden planks of the floor, and began to swing. The creaking of the hammock sounded almost musical to him, as he continued to stare at the sloth. He was trying to imagine how good it would be to live as a wild forest creature when Cícero suddenly grasped him with his right hand and stopped the hammock from swinging.

"Do you hear what I'm saying, Júlio?"

"I don't want to hear," the boy replied, threatening to get out of the hammock.

Cícero held onto his arm. He said he understood his reaction. A good boy like him could not accept the idea of killing someone. Cícero said he was proud of the fact that his nephew rejected his proposal so vehemently. But the situation was much more complex than he could imagine. Cícero had been hired to kill Amarelo. And he'd already been paid 700 cruzeiros in advance. As well as the cash, he was to receive thirty kilos of rice, twenty of beans, ten kilos of coffee, ten of sugar, five of cheese, ten cans of oil, and twelve bottles of cachaça. The payment in food and cachaça was part of an agreement between Cícero and the man who had hired him to kill Amarelo: Marcos Lima, whom Júlio also knew. Aged thirty-six, Lima had a profession that is still very common and important in the riverbank communities of the Amazon region. He was a trader who used his boat to travel and sell mass-produced goods to the inhabitants of the most isolated areas. As he did not have the 1,000 cruzeiros Cícero was demanding to kill Amarelo, Lima had suggested he be paid part of it in the food-stuffs he sold in the region.

"And all that food is going to stay here, in your house," Cícero told Júlio. "I'll take only the cachaça and the cheese."

"Uncle, I don't want to hear this. I'm not going to kill anyone. I can't even believe you're asking me to do something like that. You want me to become a killer like you? God forbid."

"You're not going to become a killer, Julão," said Cícero affectionately, taking him by the arm. "You're simply going to do this job and then you'll never have to get mixed up in anything like this ever again."

"I don't want to do it, Uncle. I don't want to."

"I know. And I think that's good. But if you don't fulfill the contract, I'll be the one who dies."

"Why's that?"

"Because Lima has already paid me, Julão. That's how things

are in this business. After you've been paid, you have to carry out the contract. Otherwise, the person who gets killed is the gunman himself. Do you want me to die?"

"Of course not, Uncle!"

"Then do as I ask."

Time went by, but their conversation got no further. Cero went on trying to convince his nephew that he had to kill Amarelo, while Júlio angrily refused to accept the idea. But Cícero insisted so much that eventually the boy began to consider the possibility of doing as his uncle was asking.

"If it was a stranger I had to kill, I might even think of doing it. But Amarelo lives as a fisherman near here. I know he is annoying and gets into lots of trouble. But just because someone is annoying is no reason to kill them. What did he do for Lima to hire you to kill him?"

"Julão, Amarelo did something very serious. Much more serious than you can imagine."

"What was it?"

Cícero explained that two weeks earlier, Amarelo had raped Lima's daughter Lúcia, who was only thirteen. One cloudy afternoon, Amarelo passed by the trader's house in his canoe. The girl was bathing in the river in a pair of shorts and a top, together with her brother José, aged seven. The motorboat Lima used was not tied up outside the store, indicating that the girl's father was away selling his merchandise. Paddling closer to Lúcia, Amarelo invited her to go with him to a nearby lake, where he said there was a family of pink river dolphins. Like nearly all the children in the region, Lúcia adored those animals. She had already seen several families, but it was always such fun to see these beautiful animals swimming in the river. As he told his parents later on,

José was also thrilled by the idea, but Amarelo said he was too young to go to the lake. Against her parents' instructions never to go near Amarelo, Lúcia got into the fisherman's canoe.

When she returned and saw her son alone on the riverbank, the thirty-two-year-old Dona Livia asked where Lúcia was.

"She went to see the dolphins, Mom," the boy replied.

"Who with?"

"With Amarelo."

Dona Livia was worried when she heard this. She told her son to get out of the water and go inside the house. Everyone in the village knew that the fisherman was interested in Lúcia. Amarelo had praised the young girl's lithe, shapely body so much that he and Lima had argued several times. Dona Livia's first thought was to take the family canoe and go in search of her daughter. But she didn't want to leave José and her youngest child Moisés, aged two, all on their own. And so she sat in the doorway to the house, praying. Without taking her eyes off the river, with the baby in her arms. She did not have long to wait: about fifteen minutes later Lúcia appeared, walking slowly, head down. Amarelo had drawn up his canoe a short distance before the village where the girl lived, and ordered her to get out and walk home.

When she met her mother—who, seeing her daughter approach, put the baby back in the hammock—Lúcia clung to her. Dona Livia asked what had happened, but the girl could not speak. Her frightened, lost look led her mother to imagine the calamity that had occurred. She led the girl down to the river, where they both waded in up to their waists. Dona Livia carefully pulled down her daughter's shorts. Lúcia was still quiet, her eyes fixed on the water. Her mother examined her daughter's clothing and saw bloodstains on the inside of her shorts.

She touched her daughter's vagina as gently as possible. Her daughter said in a strangled voice: "It hurts a lot, Mommy."

Amarelo had raped the girl in his canoe. "He told me if I didn't let him or if I cried out, he would leave me tied up in the middle of the forest for the animals to eat," said the girl. Dona Livia hugged her daughter with a strength she did not know she possessed. And she scarcely recognized herself in the overwhelming desire she felt to see someone dead. She was the one who convinced her husband to hire a gunman to kill Amarelo.

"That's what Lima told me when he said he wanted me to kill Amarelo," Cícero told his nephew.

"My God! How could Amarelo do anything so terrible, Uncle? Lúcia is such a good girl," said Júlio, who knew her from school.

"You see? That bastard deserves to die. But I'm in no state to do the job, Julão. It has to be you. If you don't, I'll be the one who dies."

Even today, Júlio Santana cannot forget how he felt that morning of August 6, 1971, as he was about to tell his uncle he would kill Amarelo. He remembers he thought over what words he would use. He didn't want to say the word "death" or any other term related to the "grim reaper." Finally Júlio thought he had hit on the right expression.

"All right, Uncle. I'll do it for you. But you mustn't ask me anything like this ever again," Júlio said sadly, avoiding his uncle's eyes.

Making a great effort, Cícero got up from his hammock. The muscles in his legs and arms were aching terribly, but he managed to walk two steps and then knelt at his nephew's feet. He took the boy's head in his big hands and kissed him on the forehead.

"I'm truly grateful, Julão. And forgive me for getting you into this. But you're the only person who can help me now."

"All right, Uncle," the boy replied. He looked away again at the sloth still clinging tranquilly and safely to its tree in the forest. *It must be great to be born an animal*, he thought. The day passed slowly by. Dona Marina and Seu Jorge were puzzled at how quiet Júlio was. Pedro and Paulo came back from class and went to play in the river. Normally, Júlio would go with his younger brothers, but that day he only left his hammock at around four in the afternoon to go for a walk in the jungle. Pedro, his thirteen-year-old brother, wanted to go with him, but Júlio said he preferred to be on his own. Because he was so close to his uncle Cícero, the whole family thought he must be sad and preoccupied because of his illness.

On the night before committing the crime, Júlio only tasted a small piece of the tender meat from the deer he had hunted the previous day, and then only at his mother's insistence. Shortly after supper, they were all asleep. Júlio found it impossible to relax. He could not stop thinking what it would be like to kill a person. However nasty and violent Amarelo was, and however much he deserved to pay for having raped such an innocent girl as Lúcia, the only one who could punish the fisherman was God. That was what Júlio had learned from his parents, who were both followers of San Jorge and went to Mass every Sunday in the village's wooden church. Whoever disobeys God is punished and goes to hell. And Júlio did not want either of those things. The idea was so disturbing that he decided to talk to Cícero about it. Climbing out of his hammock, he walked over to his uncle, treading carefully on the boards to avoid making any noise.

"Are you awake, Uncle?"

"I am. How could anyone sleep when their body aches so much?"

"Uncle, I said I'll do this job for you. But there's something that really worries me."

"What's that, Julão?"

"If I do that"—Júlio still refused to use the word "death" or anything similar—"God will punish me. And I could go to hell. I don't want to be punished or to go to hell, Uncle."

Cícero could understand his nephew's fears, and used the same argument—faith—to convince him to kill Amarelo.

"Júlão, I know that killing someone is a sin. In the same way that it's a sin to lie or to disobey your parents, as you do when you drink cachaça with me, for example. At church they also teach that it's a sin to do the things you do with Ritinha before you are married," said Cícero. Júlio lowered his eyes to the ground. His uncle went on:

"What do you do after you've disobeyed your parents, after drinking cachaça or doing naughty things with Ritinha?"

"When I get home I ask God for forgiveness," the boy replied.

"Exactly. And what do we learn in church? That you only have to ask God for forgiveness for him to grant it. Isn't that so?"

"Yes, it is."

"Well then, Julão. After you've killed Amarelo, you only have to ask God for forgiveness and he will forgive you."

"Are you sure?" the boy asked, raising his eyebrows in a frown.

"Of course! God forgives everything, Julão. Everything."

"That's right. That's what the priest said at Mass."

"Tomorrow, after killing Amarelo, you go home and pray ten Hail Marys and twenty Our Fathers. That way I guarantee you will be forgiven."

"How do you know?"

"Because that's what I do. And it always works. The person who taught me that was a priest in Imperatriz. By saying ten Hail Marys and twenty Our Fathers, you are forgiven all your sins. So now, stay calm and go to sleep."

Júlio fell asleep to the sound of rain on the hut's straw roof, silently repeating the two prayers over and over again. He wanted to be sure that on the next day after he'd carried out his uncle's instructions, he would not get a word wrong.

Unlike what happened every day without exception, Júlio awoke of his own accord, without feeling Seu Jorge push his hammock or hearing his mother calling out to him. The sun had not yet risen above the dense forest when Júlio picked up his rifle from a corner of the room, stuffed a handful of bullets into his cotton trouser pocket, and quickly put on his shirt. He stuck a knife in his leather belt, and looked across at Cícero. He did not know if his uncle was really asleep or was only pretending so as not to have to face his nephew at such a difficult moment.

"Where are you going in such a hurry?" asked Dona Marina.

"I'm going hunting, Mom," Júlio replied nervously. But Dona Marina was so busy preparing the family's breakfast—at that moment she was cooking manioc—she did not notice how agitated her son was.

Júlio rushed out of the house. In the forest he heard the frightening cries of the howler monkeys. Although they are small—an adult grows no taller than three feet—these animals produce a terrifying screech. As a young boy, their cry had always delighted him, but that morning the sound only made him all the more nervous. After walking for forty minutes through the heart of the Amazon rainforest, Júlio reached the spot where he had to wait for his victim. This was a branch of the river Tocantins that was Amarelo's favorite place to fish surubís and catfish. The fact that the fisherman had not yet arrived gave the boy a timid hope. *If Amarelo doesn't appear soon, I can go home and tell my uncle I'm not going through with it,* he thought. With every passing minute, Júlio felt more relieved. Amarelo had not appeared; God would make sure he did not become a murderer. Júlio remembers he even felt a glimmer of happiness, as if a burden had been lifted.

Propping his rifle against a tree, he lay down on the ground. He linked his hands and extended his arms as far as he could above his head. His muscles could finally relax. Looking up at the tops of the trees, he saw a spider monkey hanging from a branch. He felt as carefree as that animal. At that moment, he felt sure that God would not allow Amarelo to appear. He closed his eyes and breathed in the smell of earth still damp from the previous night's rain. He was so tired from his sleepless night that he dozed off. He woke up some time later. He had already forgotten why he was there. When he stood up he felt his shirt stuck to his sides because it was damp from the ground. Annoyed, he gave one last glance toward the river, to see whether Amarelo was there. Before that, he prayed to God: "Lord, let no one be there." His eyes pierced the forest slowly and anxiously until they settled on the yellow sand at the riverside. He was afraid to look up. But he did. No one. Nobody was fishing there. Neither Amarelo nor anyone else. Júlio felt a joy he had never before experienced. He was so excited he took off his shorts and shirt and ran toward the river. He dodged between the trees and jumped over all the roots in his way. The hot sand scorched the soles of his feet until he plunged headlong into the river, splashing water all around him. He swam for a few

minutes, then decided to return home. It was going to be difficult to confront his uncle and admit he had not completed the
task. But it was not his fault: "Amarelo did not appear," he would
tell Cícero. He got out of the water and was walking back to the
edge of the forest when he heard a gruff voice:

"What are you doing here, youngster?"

It was Amarelo, who was approaching in his canoe. Júlio
felt as if he had been struck by a bullet to the chest. He was
left speechless. He waved to the fisherman as though he were
leaving, and ran into the forest. His body was still wet, and he
found it hard to get his shorts back on. Holding his shirt in his
left hand, he slung the rifle over his right shoulder. He began to
run off back home. The rifle butt banged rhythmically on his
back as he ran. He recalled what his uncle had said: "If you don't
kill Amarelo, I'll be the one who dies." Besides, God had given
him the opportunity to return home in peace. If he had left earlier, he would not have seen Amarelo. But he had decided to
wait and now he had to keep his promise. Júlio went back deter-
minedly toward the river. It would soon be over: all he had to do
was arrive, fire a bullet into the fisherman's heart, and get rid of
the body. His uncle had also given him instructions not to leave
any evidence of the crime. After he killed Amarelo, he had to
slit open his stomach and throw the body into the river for the
piranhas to devour it. It would soon be over.

AND YET BY now he had been standing there in the thick
forest for three hours, unable to muster the courage to shoot the
fisherman. He could not take his eyes off Amarelo. With every
movement made by the man he was there to kill, Júlio thought:
Do it now. But nothing happened. On several occasions he even

rested the rifle butt on his right shoulder and looked at the fisherman's left breast. He knew he only had to pull the trigger and the job would be done. Seated in the undergrowth with the rifle across his knees, he watched the shadow of the trees sweep over the muddy waters of the river Tocantins, until the shadows were swallowed beneath the trees themselves. It was noon. Amarelo was sure not to stay there much longer.

It's now, Júlio decided.

Crouching down and hiding behind the huge trees, he took half a dozen steps toward the riverbank. Just as he did when he was hunting pacas or deer, he put his left knee on the ground and propped his right elbow on his other hip. Closing his left eye, he stared at the chest of the fisherman sitting in his canoe facing him. As he pulled the trigger, he asked God for forgiveness. At that distance—no more than forty yards—he knew he would not miss. He was so concentrated and nervous he did not even hear the gunshot. He barely saw his victim raise his hands to his chest and fall slowly, a fearful expression on his face, into the bottom of his wooden canoe. Júlio felt something he would never forget: a strange sensation of power. He had succeeded in overcoming his fear and doing what he was meant to do. Taking a man's life demanded much more courage and coolness than killing an animal. But his work was not yet finished. He had to get rid of the body.

JÚLIO WRAPPED HIS shirt round the barrel of the gun and left it propped against the same Brazil nut tree he had been leaning against. Taking off his shorts, he waded into the river, knife between his teeth. An excellent swimmer, he had no problem reaching Amarelo's canoe. Clutching the side, he peered in and saw the fisherman's dead body. His eyes were still open; his chest was drenched with blood. Júlio yanked the side of the canoe once, twice, three times until he could propel himself into it. A shudder ran down his spine when his stomach brushed the dead man's face. Spitting out the knife, he ran his hands repeatedly over his stomach in a desperate attempt to rid himself of the sensation. To no avail; but he had to finish the job.

KNITTING HIS BROW, he clenched his teeth and took hold of the knife in his right hand. He closed his eyes and stabbed again and again at his victim's stomach. He was not aware of the damage he was doing to Amarelo's corpse until he felt his hand enter the fisherman's guts. It was like sliding into muddy earth filled with worms and other disgusting creatures. He pulled his hand back out of Amarelo's abdomen and opened his eyes. Viscera and pieces of flesh were stuck to his fingers. He shook his hands desperately. He could not bear it any longer. He knelt down beside the fisherman, knees level with his waist. Shoving his hands under the body, he heaved until he saw it topple into the river. In less than a minute, a shoal of piranhas was already devouring the man he had just killed. The more his blood spread over the river Tocantins, the more piranhas came to join the first predators. Júlio used the paddle to push the body away from the canoe, then paddled to the riverbank where he had left his clothes and rifle. Before leaving, he washed out the canoe with river water to get rid of all traces of the crime: viscera, bits of flesh, and lots of blood. He hid the canoe in the forest, put on his clothes, slung his rifle over his right shoulder again, and started out toward home.

AS HE RAN through the forest, Júlio was crying in distress. A stabbing pain pierced his heart. His soul was heavy. He'd done as his uncle had asked, and yet he knew he should not have killed Amarelo. He could not stop thinking of the look of terror he had seen on the dying man's face. "It was as if he was staring at me," he told his uncle later. He had to calm down before he reached home. If his parents saw him in this state, they would be bound to suspect something. Some five hundred yards from his house, he sat down in the shade of the tall trees. Gradually his breathing returned to normal, and it was only then that he grasped the reason he was so troubled. It was the weight of the sin. He had still not said the ten Hail Marys and twenty Our Fathers—in that order—that would cleanse his soul. He threw his rifle to the ground and crept away from it. Kneeling down in the middle of the forest, he said the prayers, paying great attention not to make any mistake. When he finished the twentieth Our Father, he opened his eyes in the hope he would feel lighter. But his soul was still tormented. *It must be because I've just finished praying. It'll be better in a while*, he told himself, and headed for his house. By now it was past two o'clock in the afternoon. Dona Marina was on the riverbank, washing clothes. Seu Jorge had gone out to look for timber in the jungle. His little brothers—Pedro and Paulo—were splashing about in the river. No one saw Júlio arrive. Cícero Santana, the one who had induced his nephew to kill Amarelo, was fast asleep in his hammock. The fact that he was so relaxed upset Júlio. While he had been through the worst experience of his life, Cícero appeared to be completely unconcerned. Júlio hung the rifle behind the door and pushed his uncle's hammock with his right foot. Cícero opened his eyes.

"Well then?" he asked. "Did you shoot Amarelo?"

"I shot him, Uncle. It's done," replied Júlio.

"Did you do everything I said?"

"Yes. Everything. I even threw the body into the river for the piranhas to eat."

"Well done. What about his canoe?"

"I washed it and hid it in the forest."

"That's good, Julão. Now we can rest in peace."

"It looks as if you've been resting a good while."

"Julão, I'm sick. Have you forgotten? I'm still burning with fever and all my body is aching. I only brought you into this because there was no other way."

"All I want to do is forget this dreadful event. And don't ever come to me again to talk about killing people to make money. I don't even want to hear about that kind of thing," said the boy firmly, wagging his finger at his uncle.

"Don't worry. It won't happen again."

The hours went by, and Júlio still felt the weight of his guilt. His stomach was churning; he had no appetite. That evening, Dona Marina prepared rice and roast meat from the deer he had killed. It was Júlio's favorite dish, but he ate only two spoonfuls and went straight to his hammock. Worried, Dona Marina came over to talk to her son. He said he felt nauseous, his body was limp and his head ached. When she laid her hand on his forehead, Dona Marina quickly realized he had a high fever. "My poor boy, he's got malaria as well," she said for all the family to hear.

But Júlio did not have malaria. The fever, nausea, and pains were the signs of a nervous crisis. Soon afterward, everyone else in the house was asleep, and yet Júlio, stretched out in the hammock covered by two sheets, could not stop thinking about

Amarelo. Whenever he closed his eyes and tried to sleep, he saw the fisherman's mutilated body in front of him. For the next two weeks he could not sleep soundly. On the day of the crime, he could only manage to sleep after endlessly repeating the ten Hail Marys and twenty Our Fathers. He insisted on emphasizing one particular line from the Our Father. "Forgive us our trespasses," he begged the heavens, fists clenched. Curled up in the hammock, he made God a promise: "Never again in my life will I kill anyone, Lord. Never again."

On the Way to the Araguaia Guerrilla

TORRENTIAL RAIN WAS pouring down on the forest. It was so heavy no one dared leave the house. The straw and wood roof could not withstand the downpour that had begun the night before. Several leaks had already soaked the planks of the floor. Júlio's younger brothers Pedro and Paulo were playing a game to see which of them could catch more drops before they hit the ground. Seu Jorge and Dona Marina were stretched out in each other's arms in the same hammock. Júlio was standing in the doorway staring out at the jungle. He had never seen so much water. The sheets of rain merged with the waters of the river Tocantins to create a thick curtain. The deluge had to stop soon.

This was the morning of March 21, 1972. Júlio and his sweetheart, the fourteen-year-old Ritinha, had agreed to spend the afternoon together, all alone on a secluded channel in the midst of the forest. From their conversation two days earlier, the seventeen-year-old boy was certain that this Tuesday would be the day he had his first sexual experience. But if the rain did not stop, the romantic trip in the canoe would not take place.

Time was passing and there was no sign of the storm easing. It was time for their midday meal. Because of the rain, neither Seu Jorge nor Júlio had gone out fishing. As there was no fish, the family ate rice with egg, listening to the rain beating on the roof. Júlio wasn't hungry. Whenever he felt anxious, nervous, or sad, he lost his appetite.

"What's wrong, son? Don't you like the food?" asked Dona Marina.

"It's not that, Mom. It's just that I'm not hungry," he replied, handing her his plate.

"But you love rice with egg. Eat a little bit more. You've left almost all of it."

"I don't want it, Mom. I'll eat later."

While Dona Marina was sharing the food Júlio had left on his plate between her other two sons, he went back to the doorway. He gazed up at the sky to see if there was any trace of blue, but there was none. All he could see were dark, heavy clouds. He felt completely disheartened. How would Ritinha be feeling? Would she be as disappointed as he was? Might she also at that moment be looking up at the sky in the hope that the weather improved? Could she be as anxious as him to have sex for the first time? He sat on the ground, propped his elbows on his knees, and held his chin in his hands. Closing his eyes, he listened to the music of the rain falling on the river and the trees. It was a constant, unchanging drumming sound. An irritating sound. Nice, but deeply irritating. Júlio had always liked the rain, but this was too much. At that moment, according to what he had agreed with Ritinha, he should already be in the canoe, paddling toward the community where she lived. The journey would take about an hour.

He became more hopeful when the storm started to ease off almost an hour after their meal. Soon afterward, patches of blue sky began to appear among the clouds. But it was still raining. Much less heavily, but it had not stopped. Júlio was so anxious he told his parents he was going out in his canoe, and left the house.

"You're going to paddle in this rain, son?" Seu Jorge inquired, in that strange deep, hoarse voice of his.

"It's easing off, Dad. I can't stand being inside any longer. I'll be back soon. Bless you," Júlio responded.

"God bless you."

The journey from Júlio's house to the settlement where Ritinha lived was along the river Tocantins. On any normal day, the waters would be calm, but the heavy rain had made them rough and increased the current. This was good news for Júlio, who would paddle downstream on his way out. As he went along, he wondered what it would be like to have sex. What would he feel? Would he do everything right? His uncle Cícero Santana had told him endless stories about women, most of them prostitutes. He had even suggested taking his nephew to a brothel in Imperatriz. "Some of the girls there are beautiful. They'll drive you crazy, Julão," his uncle guaranteed him. But Júlio only wanted to "do it" with Ritinha. As he paddled, thoughts of her lovely body came into his mind. Solid, shapely legs. Her small, hard breasts fitted perfectly in his hands. He loved her big, fleshy mouth. He could spend hours kissing her. He also loved her smooth black hair that hung down as far as her waist, and her dark, round eyes. But what drove him crazy was another part of the girl's body. "Her ass is so wonderful, Uncle," Júlio always told Cícero, the only member of the family who knew he had a sweetheart. "It's firm, smooth, and round as can be."

His anxiety increased with every stroke of his paddle. He was wondering if Ritinha would be waiting for him on the riverbank as they'd agreed when he realized he had forgotten to bring the hammock to spread in the undergrowth to use as a bed. *We're going to have to do it in the canoe*, he thought. The sky was still cloudy, but the rain had ceased. In the distance he could see the first wooden houses of the riverbank village where his sweetheart lived. He took a deep breath, then exhaled until his lungs were empty. Smiling proudly, he paddled even faster. Now it was simply a matter of time. He would soon have Ritinha in his arms. Just for him. Some fifty yards before he reached her house, Júlio lifted the paddle from the water and rested it between his feet. The canoe glided on, carried by the current.

He looked to the left bank where the houses stood, but could not see his sweetheart. His sharp eyes focused on Ritinha's hut, which like all the others had been built almost a hundred yards from the river (to avoid flooding during periods of high tide, when the level of rivers in Amazonia can rise by up to eighty feet). Still no sign of Ritinha. *Can she have changed her mind?* he wondered. He scrutinized the whole village, until he spotted someone stretched out on the grass several feet from the river. He could not make out who it was, so he used the paddle as a rudder to bring the canoe to shore. It was Ritinha. She was lying on her back, staring up at the sky. There could be no other girl with a perfect body and firm breasts like her. It had to be Ritinha. He thought of calling her name, but did not want to attract attention. They had agreed she would tell her parents she was going to collect

Brazil nuts in the forest. If they saw Júlio and her leaving together in the canoe, their plan could be ruined. So to attract Ritinha's attention, Júlio beat on the side of the canoe with the paddle. She only heard him at the fourth or fifth blow. Júlio was crouched in the bottom of the canoe, with only his head visible. Ritina leapt to her feet with the most enchanting smile Júlio had ever seen. She was beautiful, with her loose, shiny black hair and bangs. She was wearing a green sleeveless blouse that revealed her strong arms, and a pair of white cotton shorts. Her lovely thighs were completely exposed. Her smooth skin as dark as açai berries excited Júlio still more than he already was. He wanted to be making love to Ritinha there and then. He wanted to hold her in his arms as quickly as possible. She started to run along the riverbank parallel to his drifting canoe. Júlio could not take his eyes off her. His heart was pounding, his breath came in excited gasps. When Ritinha was a hundred yards from her village, he steered the canoe toward the bank. He was only five yards away from her when he threw the paddle into the bottom of the canoe and leapt overboard. As the water lapped around his knees, he splashed toward his sweetheart. Ritinha greeted him with open arms and a smile that was even more beautiful than the one he had seen a few minutes earlier. They exchanged a long, moist, nervous kiss.

"Let's get away from here quickly," said Ritinha, who was worried about being seen by someone from her village.

"I forgot to bring the hammock. We're going to have to stay in the canoe," Júlio told her.

"That's fine by me. If I'm with you, I don't care where I am."

They kissed passionately again and made for the canoe. Júlio got wet to above his knees, but Ritinha's entire legs were covered. When he saw his sweetheart's thighs streaming with water, he could not contain himself, and hugged her tight. Ritinha gave him a look that Júlio loved to see on her face. "It's a mixture of happiness and slyness, Uncle," he told Cícero when he described what he saw in his sweetheart's eyes. It was only now he realized that Ritinha was not wearing a bra. Her nipples were clearly visible beneath her thin blouse. She sat in the bottom of the canoe facing him as he began to paddle for all he was worth.

TEN MINUTES LATER, Júlio steered the canoe down a narrow channel on the left-hand side of the river. The couple did not exchange a single word, and barely looked at each other. They simply smiled. Júlio could not understand why it seemed to him that Ritinha was less nervous than he was. In the channel, the rays of the sun scarcely penetrated the tops of the trees, veiling the calm waters. Júlio steered the canoe close to the bank, until he felt the hull grate on the sandy bottom. He dropped the paddle into the boat and wet his hair with river water. He also washed his face, chest, and abdomen to get rid of the sweat produced by the effort of paddling so far.

All Júlio was wearing was a pair of shorts. He stretched out his arms until he touched Ritinha's knees, and took hold of her hands. He wanted to fling himself on her and devour her, just as he'd seen alligators do with their prey half a dozen times. He was breathing so excitedly it could be heard among the cries of the toucans and macaws in the forest. Without realizing it, he pulled Ritinha toward him, teeth bared and a ravenous look in his eyes.

"Calm down, Júlio," she said. "There's no one here but us two. Nobody is going to appear and catch us. Stay calm."

"I can't bear it any longer, Ritinha. I'm going to burst," he said, slipping his hands beneath her blouse.

"Calm down," she said again, smiling as she prevented his hands from reaching her breasts.

"What's wrong, Ritinha? That's what we came here for, isn't it? Are you going to change your mind now?" he said in a voice that betrayed both annoyance and disappointment.

"No, Júlio. I'm not going to change my mind. I want this as much as you do. But I don't want it like this, with you so anxious. You haven't even kissed me since we got here."

Júlio thought perhaps there was something to his sweetheart's complaint. He was so excited he had forgotten to show the affection he himself usually saw as one of the most sublime aspects of their relationship. He pulled his hands from Ritinha's smooth stomach and lowered his eyes. He sensed Ritinha embracing him and kissing his face. He was still gazing at the bottom of the canoe when he realized Ritinha was taking off her blouse. He felt too ashamed to raise his head, but she took his hands and placed them on her breasts.

"I am yours," she whispered in his ear.

It was the longest kiss Júlio ever remembered having. Their mouths caressed each other. Their tongues seemed to be dancing for joy. He would never forget the feeling of mad pleasure he felt when he first brushed Ritinha's nipples with the palm of his hands and then squeezed them hard. He still clearly remembers how surprised he was when he felt her right hand touching him under his shorts. He wasn't expecting this kind of attitude in such a sweet girl. He was even more astonished when she gripped him firmly. His bewilderment aroused him still more. As she squeezed him with her right hand, with her left Ritinha drew his head toward her breasts.

Confused, Júlio kissed and licked Ritinha's breasts. He was

certain from her moans and panting breaths that she was enjoying all this as much as he was. He began to stroke her thighs. The moment had arrived to try to touch her where she had never allowed him to before. He hastily pushed his hand between her legs. She gave a groan of pleasure that stayed in his mind for weeks. He slid his hand inside Ritinha's shorts. For the first time ever, she allowed Júlio to touch her most intimate parts. They were wet. He had never touched a woman before, and thought she must be sweating. It was not until three days later, when he talked to his uncle Cícero, that he learned her wetness was a sign of how excited she was. His fingers caressed her. In his excitement, he pressed too hard.

"Slowly, Júlio. Slowly, or it might hurt."

He said nothing, but began to pull her shorts down. She lay back in the canoe. He pulled off his own shorts and knelt down between her legs. Her head resting on the side of the canoe, she gave him a look he could not decipher: a mixture of joy, anxiety, affection, and desire. *It must be love*, he thought. He stretched out on her body and tried to penetrate her.

"Take it gently," she said as she guided him. "Go in slowly, okay? Remember I'm a virgin."

"Me too," he added.

"Really?"

"Of course, Ritinha."

"How lovely. It'll be the first time for both of us."

The further Júlio pushed inside her, the more Ritinha cried in pain. He even asked if she wanted to stop, but her reply was to grip him tight round the waist with her legs. Despite her apparent pain, she was really enjoying it. Even so, she seemed uncomfortable in a way he could not understand. Even today,

Júlio has no idea how, pushing and pulling, she changed positions with him. He only recalls that all of a sudden he was lying there with his shoulders against the cold bottom of the canoe, with Ritinha upright on his pelvis. He felt himself penetrate her fully. It was a delicious sensation, as if she were sucking him into her. Her hands pressing against his chest, she seemed to be dancing on his lap.

Overwhelmed by a pleasure he'd never thought existed, Júlio closed his eyes and felt a gentle breeze from the forest. The movements of their two bodies made the canoe sway rhythmically. Ritinha's hands covered his face.

"Open your eyes, Júlio. Look at me," she said. He obeyed. The image he saw was marvelous. Ritinha's skin was bathed in perspiration, her skin gleaming in the timid rays of the sun that broke through the foliage. Her panting breaths and hungry look excited him even further. He felt an intense shudder run down his spine; his whole body quivered. *I'm going to come*, he thought. Clutching his sweetheart's hands, he gave a strange groan. This was the first time he had had an orgasm in a sexual encounter. But Ritinha was still aroused, moving her haunches in circular, up-and-down movements. She dug her nails into his chest, drew herself up, and then, with a long groan that was almost a sigh, collapsed on top of him. Clinging to each other, they barely heard the breeze in the trees or felt the swaying of the canoe.

They stayed like that for ten or fifteen minutes. Ritinha plunged into the stream, and Júlio did the same. They splashed about in the warm water, smiling, and then made love again. This time, Júlio was standing up, with his sweetheart's legs wrapped around his waist and arms around his chest. It was even more pleasurable than the first time. Júlio felt more at ease, more sure of himself. Ritinha appeared to feel the same. After their bath, they climbed back into the canoe and lay there for several minutes, intertwined, still naked, resting.

Then they got dressed and returned home. Júlio left the girl where he'd picked her up, saying goodbye with a lengthy kiss and a tight embrace. *This feeling must be love. That's all it can be,* he thought. He wanted to tell Ritinha he loved her, but did not have the courage. He gazed after her until she reached the doorway to her hut. As he set off back upstream, Júlio saw her standing there, giving him a discreet wave with her right hand close to her shoulder. He was so happy that he did not grow tired paddling more than an hour against the current to reach his own village. He wanted to marry Ritinha. To be with her forever. He couldn't wait to tell all that had happened that afternoon to his uncle Cícero, who was the only one Júlio felt he could talk to about it.

The conversation took place three days later. It was toward dusk on March 24, 1972, a stifling hot Friday, when Júlio, stretched out in his hammock thinking of Ritinha—whom he had not met since the day he lost his virginity—heard the sound of Cícero's motorboat.

"Uncle's here!" the boy shouted, jumping out of the hammock.

He went out to join Cícero as he was tying his boat to a tree on the riverbank. He slapped his uncle on the shoulder.

"Ritinha and I did it," he said enthusiastically.

"Hang on, my boy. I haven't properly arrived yet. What's happened?" Cícero asked, embracing his nephew.

"Ritinha and I did it, Uncle. Get it? We did that thing. In the channel in the forest near here."

"What's that? You've had her? At last? About time too," said Cícero, smiling broadly.

Again, Júlio was annoyed at the way his uncle spoke about his sweetheart.

"Don't talk like that, Uncle. I love her, and I'm going to marry her."

"I'd like to hear you tell me that in two years' time."

"What do you mean?"

"Júlio, you're like this because it was the first time you've been with a woman. Before long, you'll have others, and Ritinha will be nothing more than a memory."

"You're completely wrong. I love Ritinha. I'm going to marry her as soon as I can. I'm already plucking up my courage to talk to her father."

"And does your father know about it?"

"No," said the boy, lowering his eyes. "I want to talk to her father first. If he accepts, I'll talk to my father afterward. But now I want to tell you everything that happened."

"Between you and Ritinha?"

"Yes."

"All right, wait here. I'll say hello to your father, mother, and brothers and be right back. I've also got something I want to talk to you about."

The conversation Cícero had that evening with Júlio was to place the boy in the epicenter of the greatest armed conflict in Brazil's recent history: the Guerrilla of Araguaia.

Cícero entered his brother's house and greeted everyone with hugs and kisses. Picking up two bananas, he returned to his boat, where Júlio was waiting anxiously for him. He told his uncle all the details he could recall, including the clothes the girl was wearing that afternoon: a green blouse and a pair of white cotton shorts. "Really short shorts," he stressed. Proudly, he showed him the marks Ritinha's nails had made on his chest.

"That girl is hot stuff, isn't she?" said Cícero. "She must be delicious."

"Don't say that, Uncle. You know I don't like it when you talk that way."

After almost an hour, Júlio had still not finished describing his first sexual experience. Finally after three days he could share that unforgettable event with someone. He could have gone on all night talking about how he felt when he had Ritinha completely naked, just for him. Her skin the color of açai berries, soft and smooth. Her shiny black hair, her sturdy, shapely thighs, her plump mouth. "She's so beautiful, Uncle. She's absolutely perfect," he said, before their conversation was interrupted by Dona Marina calling out to them. Night had fallen without Júlio and Cícero realizing it.

"Come and eat, you two. Supper is ready," she shouted from the doorway.

"We're coming, Mom," replied Júlio. "You said you also wanted to talk to me, Uncle. What about?"

"Let's eat, Julão. We can talk afterward."

As soon as they had finished eating the grilled monkey meat with rice that Dona Marina had prepared, Júlio and Cícero went back to where the boat was moored. They sat down on the sand by the river and resumed their conversation.

"Julão, do you remember something I mentioned when I was here about six months ago?" said Cícero, referring to August 1971.

"When do you mean, Uncle? You're always coming here."

"That time when I was very ill with malaria."

Júlio immediately recalled how he had killed the fisherman Amarelo. He said nothing, but got up and went to the river's edge to get his feet wet.

"What's wrong, Julão?"

Staring up at the sky dotted with stars, the boy took several seconds to respond.

"Uncle, I'm not going to kill anyone, do you hear me? If you're thinking—"

"No, it's nothing like that, Julão! I'm not going to ask you to kill anyone."

"What is it then?"

"That time when I had malaria, while you were eating I mentioned the work the army was carrying out in the river Araguaia region. I told you about a friend of mine who is the police chief in Xambioá and was taking on people to help the military fight the communists hidden in the jungle. Do you remember that?"

"No, I don't," the boy replied.

"Of course you do. When I said that my friend the police chief needed men who knew their way around the jungle and were good shots, you even asked me take you along to do that work. Do you remember now?"

"No."

Júlio was still gazing up at the sky as he said this. He did not know why, but he sensed that this conversation would get him into trouble. Merely thinking about that dreadful day he killed Amarelo was enough for him to want not to be there. He had managed to free himself from the continual nightmares in which he saw the bloody corpse and the guts of the fisherman stuck to his hands. He did not want to go through that again.

"Júlio? Did you hear what I said?"

"What was that?"

"It's as if I were talking to myself. I've already asked twice. Do you want me to take you to Xambioá?"

"To Xambioá?" the boy asked nervously. "What would I do in Xambioá?"

"Are you deaf? I've just explained everything. It's as if you're on the moon."

"I'm sorry, Uncle. I was thinking about something else. What do you want to take me to Xambioá for?"

Cícero explained once again that the police chief in Xambioá was recruiting men to help the Brazilian army capture the communists hidden in the jungles of the river Araguaia region. Júlio wanted to know why the military wanted to catch these communists, and what a communist was. His uncle explained as best he could:

"Communists are people who don't accept the government's laws and want to make trouble in Brazil. That's why the army has to catch them to avoid the country becoming a real mess. Do you follow?"

"More or less," Júlio replied.

"The important thing is that we have to help the army. And I think it could be very good for you to join them, Julão."

"Why?"

"Because it's easy work and you'll earn very good money. Didn't you say you wanted to marry Ritinha? What you earn from this job will be enough to start building a little house for you two."

Júlio liked the idea. He was willing to do anything to be able to get married and live with Ritinha. Almost anything.

"Will I have to kill anyone, Uncle?" he wanted to know.

"No, Julão. Forget that stuff about killing. My friend the police chief says the army's orders are very clear. They don't want to kill anybody. They simply want to capture the communists to interrogate them and uncover their plans."

"And how would I help?"

"The army people have no idea how to find their way around in the jungle. They need someone who knows the forest well and is a good shot."

"So I'll have to shoot?"

"Possibly, if necessary. But if you have to shoot, it will only be to wound. You can trust me, Julão. That's all it will be. So we'll leave for Xambioá tomorrow, shall we?"

"I'm not sure, Uncle. I'm scared."

"Trust me, my boy. Everything will be fine. You stay with the soldiers a few days and then come home with loads of money in your pocket. They'll pay you twenty cruzeiros a day. If you stay two months with them, you'll earn twelve hundred cruzeiros [equivalent to almost six times the minimum wage of the time, which was 225 cruzeiros]."

"That's a lot of money, isn't it?" said the boy, enthusiastic at the idea of earning a wage that no one else in his community had.

"Yes, it is. Didn't I tell you it was a good idea?"

"But two months is a long time, Uncle."

"Not really, Julão. It passes by quickly. You'll even enjoy yourself. I'm sure of it. You like going around in the forest. Just imagine, you'll be guiding loads of troops. It'll be good for you."

"Will it?"

"Of course. I'll talk to your parents right now."

At first Seu Jorge and Dona Marina did not like the idea of not seeing their son for such a long time. But Cícero succeeded in convincing them to authorize their son's trip with the argument that the experience could help Júlio enter the military police. For the family, that was the best profession a boy born in the jungle could possibly have in life.

Two days later, on a Sunday, Júlio and Cícero took his boat to Imperatriz from where they would travel overland to Xambioá, on the border of Tocantins and Pará state on the river Araguaia. The boy even asked his uncle to take him to say goodbye to Ritinha, but Cícero said they would not be able to do as he wished. "We can't waste time, Julão." This was the first time Júlio was leaving the region where he lived. In a little over two hours' journey round the bends of the river Tocantins, they reached Imperatriz, where they were to spend the night at Cícero's house. Júlio was fascinated at seeing a real motorcar. Until then he had only seen automobiles in the magazines his uncle lent him. But he did not like the noise the cars made, or the crowds in the town—at that time, Imperatriz had close to fifteen thousand inhabitants. Júlio never imagined there could be so many people in one spot.

His uncle's house looked like a palace to him. It was made of wood like the one he lived in with his parents and brothers, but it had interior walls that separated the living space from the kitchen and two bedrooms. In each of them was a bed and a hammock. In the living room there was a three-seater sofa, covered in black and red checked upholstery, in honor of Flamengo, the soccer team Cícero supported. There was an enormous calendar with an image of Our Lady of Aparecida on the wall, a wooden table with four aluminum chairs. To the left of the sofa, on a bench, stood a transistor radio. In the kitchen were a woodstove and a big red box that was almost as tall as Júlio. "That's a refrigerator, Julão," Cícero explained to his fascinated nephew. *Mom would love something like that*, the boy thought. He found it delicious to drink chilled water. "It's as if your tongue goes to sleep," he said. He could not understand what the glass ball, slightly smaller than an apple, that hung from the ceiling was for. He would only find out when darkness fell.

"So it lights up all on its own? It doesn't need any kerosene?" asked the boy, whose own home was lit by two lamps.

"Julão," laughed Cícero, "it's electric energy that makes it light up. Here in the town they have an electricity generator powered by diesel. That's what makes things like the fridge and the lights work. Do you understand?"

"No. Not a thing."

"Don't worry. With time you'll learn about all that."

That night, Júlio tried to sleep in the bed, something he had never before done in his life. It was impossible. He found it strange to lie on one side or the other, and above all not to be able to swing to and fro. He got up out of the bed and went to sleep in one of the hammocks. The next morning he and his uncle hitched a ride on the truck of a local timber merchant who was going to Xambioá. Júlio was tense and silent. Cícero tried in vain to cheer him up, fooling around and telling jokes. They reached Xambioá around four in the afternoon. It was stiflingly hot. The thick red dust that the army jeeps and trucks threw up as they drove up and down irritated Júlio's eyes. These military vehicles were part of the government's battle against the movement organized by militants in the Brazilian Communist Party against the military government. At the police station, Cícero presented his nephew to the chief, Carlos Marra. He was six feet tall, dark-skinned, with muscular arms and short black hair shaved at the sides, and a round face. He also had a curious little mustache that was little more than a line above his top lip. And he had a generous belly that was always visible between the waistband of his shorts and his shirt. "He's really paunchy," the boy said to his uncle later on. Cícero and Marra greeted each other with laughter, hugs, and slaps on the chest. The police chief admired the boy's athletic build.

"Yes, Cícero. You said the boy was big and strong," said Marra, in a voice that was strangely quiet for someone that big.

"That's right. He also knows how to get around the jungle better than anyone, and he's a fantastic shot. Julão can kill a deer at a hundred yards," said Cícero, putting his arm around his nephew, who was standing there awkwardly, not saying a word, his eyes fixed on the ground.

"Great. I'm sure the kid will be very useful to us."

Carlos Marra was so impressed with Júlio that he wanted to send him to the region where the guerrilleros were that very day. He changed his mind only when Cícero asked him to.

"Marra, I'd like Julão only to go to the jungle with you. I'll be much happier if I know he's always close by you."

"What's the problem, Cícero?" the police chief asked.

"The boy is only seventeen, and he's my nephew, Marra. Have you forgotten that? If anything happened to him, my brother and sister-in-law would die of heartbreak. They've had enough with their eldest son, who left home and never came back."

"Fine. Well then, we'll leave early tomorrow morning, Julão," said the police chief, slapping the still silent Júlio on the shoulder.

"Say something, my lad," Cícero told him.

"For me, whatever you and the chief here decide is good, Uncle."

Marra, Cícero, and Júlio had lunch at a local bar. They ate tambaqui fish with rice and mashed manioc. And drank beer. Despite not liking its taste, Júlio drank two glassfuls because of the heat. While they were eating, he heard the police chief say that defeating the communists had turned out to be a far more complicated mission than the army had imagined. The military didn't even know where the guerrilleros' camps were. Beyond that, the rebels had won the sympathy and friendship of many of the region's inhabitants, who helped them by buying supplies and ammunition in towns and even hid many of them in their houses during army searches. Júlio was surprised by the fact that these communists, who according to his uncle were violent troublemakers, had nevertheless won over the local inhabitants.

"Why do people become friends with the communists when the army wants to catch them?" he asked.

"Because the communists are deceiving them, Julão," explained the police chief. "They say they're good people; but in reality they want to bring chaos to Brazil. Do you understand?"

"I understand."

"And our job here is precisely to avoid that happening."

"That's right, Julão," Cícero interrupted him. "Always stay close to Marra. And do everything he tells you. He's my friend, and he'll take care of you."

The boy said nothing, merely moving his head up and down. That night, Cícero left his nephew on his own in a boarding-house and went out, telling him he was going to drink with Carlos Marra. Júlio fell asleep thinking of Ritinha and imagining what might happen to him in this hunt for communists. *Just as long as I don't have to kill anyone*, he said to himself, in a silent prayer.

The Capture of José Genoino

THE BEATEN EARTH streets of Xambioá were deserted and silent when Júlio and Cícero left the boardinghouse at five in the morning of Tuesday, March 28. An army jeep was waiting outside. A youngster in an olive green uniform was at the wheel. The police chief Carlos Marra was seated next to him. They drove down to the river Araguaia, where a motorboat big enough for a dozen men was waiting for them. As well as the boatman—a local man who owned the boat—Júlio, Marra, and three other men went on board. Júlio reckoned that two of them were as young as him or only a few years older. None of them was wearing a military uniform, which he thought was a shame, because he would love to have that elegant green clothing, with a long-sleeved shirt and slouch hat. On the way to the riverside, he couldn't take his eyes off the driver's black boots. He would love to have a pair like that. The only shoes he had—a pair of navy blue Conga tennis shoes he got for his sixteenth birthday—were still almost new. He only wore them to go to

Mass on Sunday. He was sure Ritinha and Dona Marina would be proud to see him in boots like those.

When the motorboat set off, the first streaks of dawn were lighting the muddy waters of the river Araguaia. They were headed for somewhere near the river Gameleira. The forest there was very similar to that covering the interior of Maranhão state where Júlio grew up, with trees that grew more than 160 feet high and many branches of the main river penetrating into the jungle. His trained eyes could see that the fauna was the same as well. He managed to spot sloths, monkeys, herons, storks, and a great number of crocodiles resting on the riverbanks. But he wasn't there to see creatures of the forest. His mission was to help the police chief Carlos Marra capture the communists. According to the testimonies of local residents collected by the army, there were several guerrilleros hidden in the jungles of the region.

Marra's plan was for the group to spend a week hunting down communists in the rainforest. During that time they would sleep in army tents, and wash in rivers and streams. For the first days of the operation, they took with them five kilos of jerked meat, two tins of sausages, a one-kilo block of sugarcane, another kilo of manioc flour, and one of coarse salt. When these supplies ran out, they would eat whatever they managed to hunt and fish. From what Cícero had said about Júlio, Marra thought that his excellent aim and ability to move around in the forest would be fundamental for them to find food. They were all armed. The police chief and the other three men each had a .20 rifle and a .38 revolver. Júlio only had his .20 rifle, slung as usual over his right shoulder. On the journey to the point where they were to disembark, Marra gave them what he saw as necessary instructions.

"You have to be friendly toward the local population. They will only tell us where the communists are if they trust us. When we arrive at a village or a house, you are not to say anything. I'll do the talking. And if we find any guerrilleros, we capture them alive. We're not here to kill anyone. I want the person alive so that he can tell us where the others are hiding." When Marra said this, Júlio felt a huge sense of relief.

The week went by more rapidly than he had been expecting. And also much more quietly. In this excursion into the forest under Marra's command, Júlio felt important for the first time in his life. His mission was to find the trails people had left in the forest—and in this way they tracked down seven men, who said they were farmworkers. After the fourth day, when the supplies they had taken ran out, Júlio was also responsible for obtaining food for the group. He killed a monkey, a heron, and, on the last day, a jaguar. No one liked the muscular, nerve-filled meat, but it was all there was to eat.

In the seven days they spent scouring the jungle, they came across about ten huts. In all of them the inhabitants—natives of the region—confirmed that they had seen communists in the area, but had no idea where they were hiding. Carlos Marra's speech to them was always the same. He said that to help the communists was a very serious crime, and that anyone who collaborated with the army would be very well rewarded with money, weapons, tools, and medicines. Even so, they had no success. Lacking any physical evidence of the presence of the guerrilleros in the area, the group returned to Xambioá on Wednesday, April 5, 1972.

By the time they arrived it was dark. Júlio was even more impressed by the constant movement of military vehicles and personnel. There were people everywhere. An incredible hubbub. In the bar, music blared out of big illuminated boxes. Xambioá was completely different from the morning he left for his first operation in the Araguaia jungle. Carlos Marra took Júlio back to the boardinghouse and told him, in that calm voice of his: "My boy, you helped a lot, didn't you? If you need anything, you only have to call me." It was only later that Júlio realized he had no idea exactly how he could call the police chief if he needed to.

At the boardinghouse, he was received by the landlady, a skinny woman about five foot three, with a long, sharp nose and curly hair, whose name he never managed to find out.

"You're the nephew of the soldier from Imperatriz, aren't you?" she said, referring to his uncle Cícero, the military policeman.

"Yes I am, senhora. Why do you ask?"

"Your uncle asked me to tell you he's gone back to Imperatriz, but he'll be here on Saturday."

"And where am I going to stay?" asked the boy, looking scared and lost.

"Right here. Your uncle paid for five nights for you."

"And after that?"

"He says you are working for the army and will have the money to pay out of your own pocket."

The seventeen-year-old was disoriented. He had never needed to pay for anything from his own pocket. In fact, he had never had any money. He was frightened at being left alone in the midst of the noise and bustle of the big city. Taking the key to his room, he walked to the back of the property, where a cubicle smaller than fifty square feet with a beaten earth floor was to be his bedroom for the next few days. Worst of all was having to sleep in a bed. He thought several times of asking the landlady for a hammock, but her stony look intimidated him, and in the end he said nothing. He was so scared of having to spend the night in Xambioá without his uncle that he did not leave the boardinghouse even to eat. He cried himself to sleep, curled up in the bed with his stomach rumbling with hunger.

The next day he woke up around seven. He was very hungry, but still did not dare leave his room. He did not know anyone in the town, and wished his uncle Cícero were there. At one point he opened the door a crack and looked out. He saw a man walking toward the entrance to the boardinghouse and thought of doing the same, to speak to the landlady. But he didn't have the courage. He lay down on the bed again, and cried a second time. He would have given anything to be back in his own house, in the peace and quiet of the Amazon rainforest, on the banks of the river Tocantins. That was where he belonged. He was still in tears when he heard three or four knocks on the wooden door. A loud voice sounded outside.

"Wake up my boy, wake up!" It was the landlady.

"I'm already awake," Júlio replied, after a few moments of not knowing what to say.

"It's almost noon. You haven't been out since yesterday. The chief left you some money."

Júlio brightened. With money, he could go out to eat and overcome his dreadful hunger. When he opened the door the landlady handed him 140 cruzeiros in notes tied with a red nylon band. It was payment for his seven days' work in the Araguaia jungle. Júlio had never seen so much money in his life. He had no idea what he could do and buy with all that. He thanked the landlady, who seemed to him far more pleasant than on the previous day.

"How much do you think I need to take to eat?" he asked.

"Do you mean money? How much money will you spend on eating?"

"Yes, senhora. How much?"

'My boy, with ten cruzeiros you'll be able to eat until you burst," she replied.

Júlio took ten cruzeiros from the bundle of notes and put it in his shorts pocket. He rolled the rest of the money in a piece of paper he found on the floor of the room, wrapped it up, and slipped it inside his underpants. Nothing would make him let go of that packet. He put on his shorts and left the boardinghouse. As he walked down the street he saw something he would never forget. It looked like an enormous iron monster, shaped like a dragonfly. The most incredible thing about it was that it had no wings. *How can that contraption fly?* he wondered. He had already seen planes scouring the skies above the forest. And this was definitely not an airplane. He gazed after the monster until it disappeared over the horizon. In a bar about two hundred yards from the boardinghouse he ate sticky rice with beans and roast chicken. Dona Marina's rice was infinitely tastier. With the meal he drank two cans of Coca-Cola. As he ate, he could not help thinking of the strange object he had just seen flying above Xambioá. He was paying for the lunch—at four cruzeiros, he even thought it was cheap—when a youngster in an army uniform came up to him.

"Are you the nephew of Cícero the military policeman?"

"Yes," said Júlio, pleased to be speaking to someone who knew who he was.

"The chief is waiting for you at headquarters. Let's go."

Júlio spent the rest of the afternoon going around the town with Marra. He learned that the military personnel overrunning

Xambioá belonged to the three branches of the armed forces: army, navy and air force. They were all there to fight the communists. He saw the makeshift military bases they had made. The soccer field had been transformed into a landing strip with a big tent that could fit up to thirty men and which functioned as a field station and a barracks for recruits. It was there that he learned that the flying monster was called by the complicated name of *helicopter.* "One day, you'll fly in one of those things as well," the police chief told him. Although he was intrigued by the idea, Júlio did not know if he would have the courage to get into that extraordinary machine.

OVER THE FOLLOWING five days, Júlio's routine was almost always the same. He spent most of his time walking round the town, usually on his own. He had still not got used to the intense traffic of military jeeps and trucks. Every day he paid a ten- or fifteen-minute visit to Marra at the police headquarters, to find out if the date for their next incursion into the jungles of Araguaia had been fixed. At dusk one day he was near the landing strip watching a helicopter land. He could not understand how it could hover so elegantly without wings. He approached to see it come down at close hand for the first time. The helicopter was about thirty feet above the ground when its rotors threw up a cloud of thick red dust. Júlio closed his eyes in pain and tried to keep off the dust by waving his hands. He was coughing nervously. The taste of earth in his mouth was new to him. He carried on salivating and spitting painfully almost until he reached the boardinghouse almost twenty minutes later.

On the journey from the military base to his lodgings, he stopped at a bakery and bought four French loaves, a half pound of cheese, and two cans of Coca-Cola. This was his supper every night. To drink two Coca-Colas was a luxury he had never enjoyed back in Porto Franco. His parents always told him there were more important things to buy, such as beans, salt, sugar and oil. "Coca-Cola is for the rich," Seu Jorge would repeat. Now, thanks to the work he was doing for the army, Júlio could drink as many cans as he liked. He felt rich, and yet he was still sad. Not a night went by when he did not think of Ritinha. He would give anything to see his sweetheart, or at least talk to her. He could not get her plump mouth, firm breasts, smooth hair, and shapely ass out of his mind. He was convinced that Ritinha missed him as well. But there was a point to all his suffering. After he had finished his work in Araguaia, he would go back to his native region with enough money to marry Ritinha.

The next morning, he was woken up by loud knocks that seemed to want to break down the wooden door. He recognized Carlos Marra's voice.

"Come on, Julão! Get up, boy! It's six o'clock already," shouted the police chief.

"Coming," replied Júlio, jumping out of bed bewildered as to what Marra was doing there so early in the morning.

It was April 11, 1972, a Tuesday. Exactly one week later, Júlio Santana was to take part in an episode that would go down in the history of Brazil: the capture of the guerrillero José Genoino Neto, who a decade later would be elected to the federal parliament representing the Workers' Party for São Paulo, and would become one of the most influential and respected politicians in the country.

Wakened by the chief's shouts, Júlio picked up a plastic bag with a change of clothes—a pair of shorts and a shirt—and left the room eating half of a loaf left over from the previous evening. Out in the street, a jeep was waiting with the engine running. Júlio did not like the expression on Marra's face. He was still settling on the backseat when Marra said:

"Julão, if you really want to do this work with us, you have to be more responsible."

"I don't understand, sir," he replied, wiping the sleep from his eyes as the jeep set off.

"I said you had to be ready at half past five. We reached your lodgings at six and you were still asleep. That won't do."

"But you didn't tell me anything, sir."

"I sent Private Santos to tell you."

"Then go and complain to him. Because no one gave me any message, no sir. I don't even know who Private Santos is."

When he heard this, Marra ordered the driver to go back to headquarters. When they arrived, he jumped out of the jeep and told Júlio to do the same. They went inside. Sure that the chief had already left for the jungle, the soldier was sitting with his feet up on the wooden desk. When he saw Marra enter, Santos leapt up and gave a military salute.

"Where do you think you are, soldier? Do you think you're at home?" Marra reproached him.

The soldier did not reply, but lowered his head. The chief went on:

"What did I ask you to do last night?"

"To go to the boardinghouse and leave a message for Cícero's nephew," said the soldier, still staring at the ground.

"That's right. I've just left the lodgings and know you didn't even turn up there. The kid didn't even know he was supposed to be ready at half past five. Now tell me, what am I supposed to do with you?" Even though he was obviously angry, Marra still spoke in that calm voice of his.

"I don't know, sir."

"Well, I do. You're under arrest until I return from the jungle. Then you vanish from here. I don't want to see your face in Xambioá ever again."

"But chief, I—""I don't want to hear, you asshole. And if you talk any more nonsense, it'll be the worse for you."

Even though Carlos Marra was always stern, Júlio had not imagined he could be so harsh, cruel even. To put Private Santos in jail and then make him leave Xambioá simply because he had forgotten to pass on a message seemed to him too heavy a punishment. But he was not there to question Marra's decisions. There was something else that intrigued him.

"Chief, why did Private Santos give you a military salute? Isn't that only for the army?" he asked.

"That's right, Julão," replied Marra with a smile. "The thing is, I'm also part of the military. I'm a sergeant in the army."

"Is that so? So why don't you wear a uniform?"

"Because I don't like to and it's not necessary for the work I do here in Xambioá. In our operations in the jungle, wearing a uniform could scare the people living there. That's why I prefer to dress as a civilian."

"That's interesting. I'd give anything to be able to wear one of those uniforms."

"Is that so? When you leave Xambioá I'll give you one."

"Are you serious?" asked the boy, leaning forward from the backseat of the jeep and bringing his face close to Marra's left shoulder.

"Of course. You can count on me."

When they reached the banks of the river Araguaia, the same boatman was waiting for them as a week earlier, sitting in the same motorboat. With him were four men. The three who had taken part in the first mission: Ricardo, Emanuel, and Forel, and another one, who from his graying hair and the wrinkles around his eyes Júlio took to be between thirty and forty years old. "Julão, this is Tonho," said Ricardo. They greeted each other with a nod of the head. In the journey to the region of the river Gameleira, the group talked about women, soccer, and communists. Tonho did not speak. He laughed a great deal and showed interest in what the others were discussing, but never gave his opinion. He was an almost bald, muscular black man with bulging eyes, a long nose, and arms that caught Júlio's attention. "That guy's arm is about twice as thick as mine," he commented to the chief. Tonho's silence intrigued him so much that he asked Ricardo if the new member of the group was mute. "No, he can talk. You'll find out why he's so quiet before long," said Ricardo, chuckling loudly.

There was a big sack in the boat containing their supplies: five kilos of dried meat, two tins of sausages, a kilo block of sugarcane, a kilo of manioc flour, two of rice and one of coarse salt. According to Marra's plans, their mission would end on April 17. They would be searching for communists for six days. In addition to the supplies and weapons they also took several different kinds of medicines, and half a dozen army shirts, all of them long-sleeved. The medicines and clothing were to be used to convince the people living in the region to pass on information about the whereabouts of the guerrilleros.

On the first night of their operation, Júlio discovered the reason for Tonho's silence. After they had put up the tent they were to sleep in, they all went to bathe in the river except for

Tonho, who was preparing their dinner: rice with dried meat. Ashamed of being seen with no clothes on, Júlio was always the first into the water and the last to leave. As the group began to eat, Tonho went to bathe in the river. Júlio was just clambering out of the warm water. Tonho was a few yards from him when the chief shouted from thirty yards away in the jungle.

"Tonho, bring me my watch. I forgot it down there," said Marra.

"Where is it, chief?" asked Tonho, in a squeaky, high-pitched voice.

"Close to a big rock, on the left of the track."

"Okay, I'll bring it after I've bathed."

In addition to his squeaky voice, Tonho had another problem: he had a bad lisp. It made Júlio want to laugh, but he didn't want to upset his colleague. He had never heard any man with such a strange, funny voice, let alone someone as big and strong as Tonho. When he pronounced the letter "b," it sounded very like an "m." "He quacks like a duck," Júlio commented to Ricardo later on.

Biting his lip to disguise how much he wanted to laugh, Júlio got out of the water, hastily put on his shorts, and ran toward the camp, not even daring to look at Tonho. In the tent, he took the shirt he had just washed and stuffed it into his mouth. That way he could laugh as much as he wanted without attracting the group's attention. He laughed so much that tears rolled down his cheeks. Forel, who was eating outside with the others, heard a strange sound coming from the tent and came to look. He thought the boy was crying. "What's wrong, kid? Why are you crying?" he asked. That was too much for Júlio to bear. He pulled the shirt out of his mouth and laughed as he had rarely laughed in all his life. He curled up on the ground in a fetal position, clasping his stomach. "Oh, my God, my god!" he gasped between one burst of laughter and the next.

"What's going on in there, Forel?" asked Marra.

"Nothing, sir. Apparently the boy heard the way Tonho speaks. The poor kid can't stop laughing," said Forel.

He tapped Júlio on the head and before rejoining the others eating close to the fire, warned him:

"Make sure you do all your laughing now. If you laugh in front of Tonho, he'll tear you apart."

Not even this warning could make Júlio contain himself. He went on laughing until he was too weak to carry on. From that night on, he made sure not to come face to face with Tonho. He never said a word to him and moved away whenever he threatened to speak.

Over the next five days, the group's routine did not change. Whole days walking through the dense jungles of the river Araguaia in unbearable heat and constantly attacked by swarms of insects. They talked to different inhabitants in the region—most of them peasant farmers—and even bribed some of them with medicines and clothes. A lot of them promised to keep an eye out for the communists and to help in future operations. But for the present, they said they knew nothing.

By Sunday, April 16, the squad's supplies had run out. The men were exhausted, and disheartened that their work had produced no results. They had not seen a single guerrillero. Júlio, who was guiding the team through the forest, was beginning to think the story about communists was nothing more than idle gossip. As night fell that day, on orders from Chief Marra, Júlio led the group to the house of Pedro Mineiro, a peasant farmer who owned land in the region. They had already been there two days earlier, and were going to eat and spend the night at his house. He was one of those who had agreed to collaborate with the army in their search for communists. On the way there, Marra caught his left foot in a tree root and afterward found it hard to walk. Pedro Mineiro was born in Minais Gerais state, but had lived in the river Gameleira region for almost ten years. Aged forty-two, well over six foot, he had fine fair hair swept back and a skinny build. His long, pointed chin made his face look triangular. On his farm he kept half a dozen cows and a few pigs and chickens.

"Hi there, Mineiro," said Marra as he approached the wooden house where the farmer lived with his wife and two small children.

"Hallo, chief. Are you looking for shelter?" asked Mineiro, guessing what Marra wanted.

"That's right. It'll soon be nightfall and we're dead tired and hungry. Are you able to help?"

"Of course. You know you can always count on me."

"Thank you, Mineiro."

"It's nothing. Will you give me another of those army shirts of yours? They're wonderful for getting through the jungle."

"Of course. The next time I'm here, I'll bring two pairs of shorts and two shirts for you."

That night they ate chicken stew with potatoes and rice. Júlio ate three platefuls. During the meal, Carlos Marra commented that he and his men would be returning to Xambioá next morning. But Pedro Mineiro said something that made him change his mind.

"I think you ought to stay a few more days," said Mineiro.

"Why's that?" asked Marra.

"A friend of mine told me he saw some guerrilleros over by

Bandas dos Caianos," said the farmer, referring to a small village in the area.

"When was that, Mineiro?"

"Only yesterday, chief. That's what I'm saying. If you and your men searched in the jungle right away you could catch those bastards."

"If I decide to stay a few more days, will you house and feed us? I'll pay for everything later."

"Of course, chief. And there's no need to pay anything. You know I'm here to help get rid of those communists."

Marra and his group slung their hammocks on the terrace of Mineiro's house. Shortly before they went to sleep, Marra reminded them that if they came across any guerrillero in the jungle they should not, whatever happened, shoot to kill. The objective was to capture the communists in order to interrogate them. That was the only way they could find out where the movement's support bases were so that the army could then completely wipe out the guerrilleros. "So you are to fire only if you are completely sure you're not going to kill anyone," he told his men.

AT SEVEN O'CLOCK the next morning, Carlos Marra decided to test their marksmanship. He wanted to know which of them was the best shot. They placed a kitchen oil can at twenty yards' distance, and fired at it one by one. Whoever missed was eliminated. In the first round, they all hit the target. When the distance was increased to twenty-seven yards, Forel and Ricardo missed. The contest continued between Júlio, Emanuel, and Tonho. At thirty-two yards' distance Emanuel, who was the first to fire, missed. Júlio had drawn the second turn. After telling them so many stories about his hunting trips in the forest when he killed animals that were more than fifty yards from him, he did not want to miss now. Besides that, he felt obliged to prove to the police chief that he had not made a mistake in recommending him for this job.

He pressed the wooden rifle butt against his right shoulder. He inhaled deeply, then held his breath. He squeezed the trigger and saw the can go flying from the branch it had been on. He inhaled, then breathed out, relieved and proud. Tonho also hit the target. The can was placed at thirty-eight yards from the remaining two shooters. Júlio was to go first. Until now, he had fired the rifle standing up. Now he asked Carlos Marra if he could kneel down as he did when he was hunting. "My boy, if you hit the target, you can shoot standing on your head," the chief replied, and everyone laughed. Júlio placed his left knee on the ground and propped his right elbow on his right hip. Closing his left eye, he stared at the center of the can. Without knowing why, he remembered the day he had killed Amarelo, eight months before. When he peered at the can, he saw the fisherman's bloody body in front of his eyes. The dense jungle that was like a green wall behind the can reminded him of the spot where he had killed Amarelo. He had to calm down: he knew that if he fired in that state, he was bound to miss. The more he tried to be calm, the more nervous he became. He had already been kneeling down, staring at the can for two or three minutes, when he heard: "Holy mother of god! The boy's become paralyzed . . ." said Tonho in that shrill, lisping voice of his. Try as hard as Júlio could, he could not contain himself. He threw the rifle to ground and burst out laughing. Standing six feet behind him, Tonho was hopping mad. "Are you laughing at me?

Are you laughing at me?" he said. Júlio could not stop laughing. He lay on the ground clutching his belly and writhing around as he laughed and laughed. Tonho was even more annoyed when he realized that the rest of the group was smiling as well.

"Leave that idiot laughing, I'll shoot first," said Tonho, bending down to pick up the rifle Júlio had left on the ground.

"No. I'm going first," said the boy, stretching out his arm to grasp the rifle butt, still laughing. He found Tonho's way of speaking so strange and funny that he no longer thought about the day he had committed the first murder in his life. Controlling his laughter, he settled back into his previous position. He stared at the can and fired. His aim was good. He heard Marra comment some feet behind his back: "This kid is really good. Just as Cícero said." Júlio was pleased to hear this praise. Irritated at the way his companions had laughed, Tonho quickly took the weapon, aimed, and fired. The can did not move. "I only missed because of that jerk who was getting on my nerves," he complained. "He's a—" But before Tonho could curse the boy, the police chief interrupted him.

"Men, come over here," he said. "I want you to pay attention to what I'm going to say. Since we've proved that Júlio is the best shot in the group, if we find any communists and have to shoot, the one who fires first will be the boy."

"But chief—" complained Tonho.

"No ifs or buts, Tonho. That's how it is. End of story. And heaven help anyone who disobeys. Julão shoots first. If he misses, you'll all get your chance. I don't want to see anyone complaining or making a face. We have to work together and help each other."

Júlio listened to all this proudly, his eyes fixed on the ground.

AFTER THE TARGET practice, Marra and his group had breakfast and left Pedro Mineiro's house. As they were leaving, the police chief gave the farmer an order: "Tell the Army I need a helicopter tomorrow, first thing in the afternoon. If I'm not here at your house, they should search for me and my men in the forest." Mineiro did not ask any questions, but simply said he would do as Marra asked. Júlio listened to their conversation in silence, but was curious to know why Marra wanted the helicopter.

"My foot is killing me, Julão. I don't want to spend another two days walking through the forest to reach Xambioá. In a helicopter we can get back quickly and without any effort," Marra told him.

"If I want to, will you let me go back that same way we came, walking and then by boat?" the boy asked. This brought a smile to the police chief's face.

"Of course, kid. You can do as you wish. But I promise that there's no danger in traveling by helicopter. Trust me."

"Of course, chief, of course."

"And besides . . . I don't even know if the helicopter will turn up. It could be that Mineiro isn't able to pass on the message to the army, or they might not have a helicopter available."

"God willing."

In case they had to sleep in the rainforest—something none of them wanted to do—they took their hammocks and a big iron cooking pot full of rice, manioc meal with egg and pieces of cooked jerky. In his knapsack Tonho also brought a little coffee, a handful of coarse salt, half a dozen limes, and three tins of sardines that Pedro Mineiro had given the squad. Marra was riding a horse the farmer had lent them. Júlio knew that with his great belly, Carlos Marra wouldn't be able to spend the whole day in the dense forest as they had agreed. At around two in the afternoon, they found fresh footprints close to the river Gameleira. From the size of the prints and the distance between them, Júlio deduced they were made by a man almost six feet tall. The fact that this person was wearing shoes attracted Marra's attention. "People here in the region usually go through the jungle barefoot," he said.

They followed the tracks, which were heading away from the river Gameleira. Every so often, the dense forest and dried leaves strewn on the ground made Júlio's task very difficult. When that occurred, he used other signs such as snapped-off or twisted branches as proof that someone had been through there. Farther on, he again came across the footprints of the man they were pursuing.

Around four in the afternoon, a light rain began to fall, creating yet another problem. The rainwater would soon erase the tracks. In order not to lose the trail or at least to get as close as possible to the suspect, Júlio sped up. Less than half an hour later, Marra complained he was exhausted.

"No one can keep up with you, Julão," he said.

"I can," protested Tonho.

Júlio was so focused on the trail that he didn't even find his colleague's fluty voice funny.

"Chief, can I make a suggestion?" asked Júlio.

"Of course, Julão."

"You stay here with the others and I'll follow the tracks to see if I can find this person. Then I'll come back and tell you what I found."

'I'm not sure, kid. What if you catch up with him and he turns out to be the communist?'

"That's no problem. I'll tell him I live in the region. I'll say I'm a nephew of Mineiro's. Then I'll come back and we can all follow him," said Júlio with calm assurance.

"Good, Julão. I like it. You keep on his trail. While you're doing that, we'll set up our hammocks and make a fire to cook the food. Don't be too long. If you think the guy is a long way off, come straight back."

"That's fine, chief," said Júlio, and started to run off into the forest. He had time to hear Ricardo comment: "That boy is like a dog chasing a bone."

Júlio ran as he had learned to do ever since he was a small boy in the jungles of Porto Franco. First he looked ahead and studied the position of the trees for the next ten yards. Then he looked down at the ground, searching for footprints and big roots that could trip him up. He was absolutely certain that the man he was following could not move as quickly as he did. He was determined only to return to the place where Marra and the other men had made camp with the news that he had found the suspect. The rain was still falling softly and insistently. The damper the ground became, the more difficulty he had in identifying the trail left by the person he was pursuing. Night was falling when he spotted a clearing about two hundred square feet in the midst of the jungle, with a hut made of wood and palm leaves in its center. When he saw there was no one inside, apart from a dog lying under a wooden bench, Júlio kept on going. Less than a mile farther on, he came to a village with half a dozen houses. In the first, a man with graying hair was leaning out of a window lighting a corn cigarette. The feeble light from the lamp hanging from the ceiling was not strong enough for Júlio to clearly make out the man's face. Before he could speak to him, the old man said in a gruff voice:

"Come in out of the rain, boy. You'll catch a cold."

"I can't. I'm looking for a friend of mine," replied Júlio, flicking the rainwater from his eyes and running his fingers through his wet hair.

"You have a friend here?"

"He's not from here. We were hunting and I got separated from him."

"Hunting? How come you were hunting without a weapon, boy?"

It was only then that Júlio realized that in his hurry he had left his rifle where the police chief and his men had made camp. He did not know what to say. He stared at the man not knowing what to say. Ashamed, he looked down at the ground.

"Young man, you don't have to lie to me," said the old man, making Júlio look up sharply.

"What do you mean?" he said.

"I know what you want. You want to know about your friend the communist, don't you?"

Júlio found it impossible to react. It was as if his mind was blocked.

"One of those communist lads passed through here about twenty or thirty minutes ago. He was asking if anyone knew where the people from São Paulo who are at Dos Caianos were."

Júlio knew that "people from São Paulo" was how the locals in Araguaia referred to the guerrilleros, because that was the city many of them came from. But he had no idea what "Dos Caianos" meant. And he couldn't ask, because that would show the old man he was not part of the movement against the military dictatorship.

"Yes, you're right. That's the one. I'm sorry I lied. Do you know which direction my friend went in?" said Júlio.

"No, my boy. Since no one could tell your friend where the people from São Paulo were, he went back into the jungle and vanished."

"Which direction did he take? Did you see him?"

"He went in the direction you came from. If the forest wasn't so big, I reckon you two would have run into each other," said the old man.

"Thank you. You've helped a lot. Just one more thing."

"Tell me."

"Can you give me a glass of water?"

After slaking his thirst, Júlio headed back, running even more quickly than he had on the way there. He was worried that the communist would reach the spot where his friends were and catch them by surprise. Or that the group might capture the guerrillero without him. Despite the almost complete darkness, he ran through the forest without difficulty, recognizing every inch of the way. Although his body was calling out desperately for him to stop and urinate, he kept going until he reached the spot where Marra and his men were camped. Contrary to what he had imagined—and strangely, even hoped for—he did not meet the communist on the way. But he felt satisfied, and proud of himself. He was bringing information he thought would be very useful for the chief. He told his story to the group enthusiastically. He spoke standing up, waving his hands and arms in the air. He stressed how good he was in the forest, running through the jungle like a jaguar. And he said something that left them even more excited than they already were.

"I think that guy is going back to where he came from. I think he's going to pass close to here."

"What if he's already done so? What if he ran the whole way like you?" asked Emanuel.

"I doubt it," Júlio said. "He doesn't know he's being followed. And even if he did, I doubt if he can run as fast as me."

"I'm not sure," said Emanuel.

"Men are like animals, Emanuel. They only run if they feel they're being followed or are in danger. And since that communist doesn't know we're on his trail, he must be very relaxed. He's probably stopped to sleep, and he'll set off again tomorrow," said the boy, with a firmness that surprised even him.

"I think the boy is right," said Marra. "Let's eat and try to sleep. We'll wake up really early tomorrow morning."

Carlos Marra and his group were already on their feet shortly before 5 a.m. on the morning of April 18, 1972, a Tuesday. Tonho made a fire to heat the coffee. They ate rice with manioc meal and jerky, took the hammocks down, and threw everything into a big sack. Then they set off again in pursuit of the guerrillero. Marra accepted a suggestion by Emanuel and ordered his men to spread out in a line, leaving about sixteen feet between them. That way they would cover a much wider area than if they advanced single file. Ricardo was on the far left, leading the horse on a rope. As Marra thought Júlio knew the jungle best, he put him in the center and took up his own position on his right.

The ground was still damp from the previous night's rain. Júlio loved the smell of wet forest. He felt at home there. His eyes scanned every inch of the jungle. He heard something in front of him, to the left. He raised his left arm. This was the agreed signal for the men to come to a halt. He pointed in the direction from which the sound only he had heard had come. Turning the palms of his hands downward, he signaled to the others to crouch down. He squatted and went forward with slow, silent steps. Looking back, he signaled with his right hand for Marra to come up to him. When he was close by, the boy pointed to behind a hundred-foot-tall mahogany tree. The chief said he couldn't see anything. Júlio pointed again: it was a big tapir.

"Why would I want to know about a tapir?" complained Marra.

"I just wanted to show you. So that you know I can see everything. If it had been that communist, I would have seen him," the boy explained.

"All right. But forget about the animals. I want you to find that sonofabitch."

It was not long before the chief's wish was granted.

Less than thirty minutes later, around six in the morning, Júlio raised his left arm again. They all halted. He glanced at Marra and whispered: "I can see someone up in front of us." Marra limped over to him. The man was walking along a track about a hundred yards ahead of them. He was wearing a pair of dark shorts and a light-blue long-sleeved shirt, rolled up above his elbows. He was skinny, about six feet tall. He had short, unkempt hair and a scrawny beard in a thin, square face. He was carrying a plastic bag in his right hand. He was walking along slowly, which Marra took to mean he was not anxious. "Just as you said, Julão. He hasn't the slightest idea he's being followed."

They followed him until they reached a spot where there was less vegetation: this was the moment to confront him. Marra, Júlio, and Emanuel were in front. As they came up to the man, Marra said to Júlio: "I know that face." The boy was confused: how could the chief know a communist who was in the middle of the jungle? But there was no time to ask him.

"Good morning, Geraldo," said Marra is his usual calm tone. The man turned in surprise.

"Good morning, chief. What are you doing in these parts?"

Marra and Geraldo knew each other from Xambioá. Every so often, Geraldo, a twenty-five-year-old youngster, would appear in town to buy supplies and ammunition for his rifle and revolver. He told everyone he was a farmer. He had been living in a straw-roofed wooden hut on the banks of the river Gameleira for two years.

Born in Quixeramobim, in the interior of Ceará state, Geraldo was in fact José Genoino Neto, a student of philosophy and law at the Ceará Federal University, a member of the Communist Party of Brazil who gave up his life in Fortaleza to join the armed movement fighting the military dictatorship. He was one of the around seventy guerrilleros who were operating in the jungles of Araguaia. His false identity was essential for him to be able to circulate among the inhabitants of the region without being identified as a communist or arrested by the army. His northeastern accent was a great help in this.

"We're looking for a communist who's in these parts," said Marra.

"You know I have nothing to do with things like that. I'm only a farmer," said Genoino.

"I think you're mixed up with those communists. Come with us. We're going back to Xambioá and I want you to come too."

"Why are you doing this to me?"

"If you've done nothing wrong, you've no need to worry. Ricardo, tie him up," ordered Marra.

Ricardo tied Genoino's hands with one end of the rope. He gave the other end to Marra, who mounted his horse and pulled the guerrillero behind him along a track through the jungle. Júlio,

Ricardo, Emanuel, Tonho, and Forel were walking in front of the horse. They were pleased to be going back to Xambioá. They were tired of spending day after day in the rainforest, attacked by swarms of insects, sleeping in the forest, with poor food.

But five minutes after he had been tied up, Genoino managed to yank the rope out of Carlos Marra's hand. His hands still tied, he ran toward the dense jungle. The chief called on him to stop once, twice, three times. Without success.

"I'll tell them to shoot, Geraldo," he shouted.

"Go ahead," replied Genoino, not looking back.

Marra gave Júlio a sharp tap on the shoulder.

"Julão, bring that bandit down."

"What do you mean?" asked the boy.

"Shoot him now, before he escapes. But remember I want him alive."

Júlio quickly reached for the rifle slung across his shoulder and knelt down. He put his left knee on the damp ground and steadied his right elbow on his other leg. He had the man in his sights. But Genoino was zigzagging as he ran, and Júlio did not want to miss or, worse still, kill the communist. The fugitive carried on running. Marra asked Júlio nervously if he was going to fire or let him get away. The boy said nothing. He stared at Genoino's back, just below his chest on the right-hand side, and waited for what he considered to be the perfect moment to shoot. He had to wait for the precise instant when the guerrillero was not shielded by any tree.

Closing his left eye, Júlio inhaled until he felt his lungs were full, then held his breath. As he pulled the trigger, he saw his target move to the left. The bullet grazed his right shoulder.

Genoino felt as if his arm had been sliced by a knife. He was so stunned he was not sure what had happened. Dropping the plastic bag, he raised his left hand to the wound. The shirtsleeve was already wet with blood. Panting, he ran on twenty yards, then fell into a thicket, hoping to hide from his pursuers. With his eyes closed and teeth clenched from the pain, he pulled some bushes and leaves over his body. Even after he had fired, Júlio did not move, his eyes fixed on the fugitive.

"Did you hit the sonofabitch, Julão?" asked Carlos Marra.

"Yes I did, sir," the boy replied. "He fell in the middle of the jungle."

"Let's go get the bastard."

They found the young guerrillero cowering in the undergrowth, pressing his wound with his left hand, writhing in pain. Marra told Tonho to go and pick up the bag Genoino had been carrying, and approached the communist.

"A farmer wouldn't run away, Geraldo. Does that mean you're a communist?"

"I'm a farmworker, chief," said Genoino.

"We'll see about that. I want to see how long you're going to lie."

Tonho interrupted them, bringing the guerrillero's plastic bag. Inside were a shirt, snakebite antidote, a little flour and salt, plus a .38 revolver. For Carlos Marra, the weapon was a strong indication that Genoino was involved with the rebel movement.

"Shall I tie him up again, chief?" asked Ricardo.

"Yes, tie him, but with his hands behind his back."

They continued along the track. Carlos Marra was on horseback and the five men were surrounding José Genoino. Since Júlio had told them about the hut he'd seen the previous night, Marra ordered the boy to guide them there. It took them almost half an hour. Inside the hut they found an iron cooking pot, two hoes, a wooden bench, some leftovers, and traces of gunpowder. Marra was sure the hut was one of the support bases used by the communists.

"Do you know this place, Geraldo?" he asked.

"No, sir. I've never been here," Genoino lied.

"This is the communists' lair, isn't it?"

"I don't know, sir. I told you, I don't know."

Carlos Marra did not believe the prisoner. And he became certain he was lying when the dog that was in the hut came over to the young guerrillero, wagging its tail and starting to lick his feet. The mongrel, with straggly reddish fur and droopy ears, had given José Genoino away. Everything was clear now to the police chief. The farmer he knew by the name of Geraldo was in fact a communist. End of story. Now he would use all the means at his disposal to drag the information he wanted out of him. This was the start of what José Genoino today considers the worst moments of his life. Moments that remained forever marked in his memory and on his body.

Certain he was part of the guerrilla, Marra asked him about the whereabouts of the armed movement's other bases, essential information if they were to defeat the rebel group. He also wanted to know how many guerrilleros were active in the river Araguaia region, what weaponry they had, how they communicated with one another. Genoino's answer to all these questions was the same: "I don't know." Marra decided that the best way to get him to talk was by torturing him. They began to beat him up, kicking and punching him all over the body. Genoino felt a dreadful pain in his stomach and the bitter taste of blood in his mouth. His hands were still tied behind his back. He hunched up, trying to protect himself, and covered his chest with his elbows.

Marra himself did not touch the communist. He stood there, giving orders. Júlio also stayed out of the beating. He told the chief he did not want to take part, and spent the whole time sitting on the ground, clutching his rifle. At every blow Genoino suffered, the boy grimaced in pain. He could not understand how Ricardo, Emanuel, Tonho, and Forel, whom he had lived with for the past seven days, appeared to be finding pleasure doing this. It was after midday by the time the men stopped beating their prisoner. Genoino lay unconscious on the leaves strewn on the ground, his body smeared with mud. Marra ordered Tonho to cook the men something. Their lunch consisted of the leftover rice and manioc meal, with three tins of sardines. They all ate sitting on the ground, scooping the food from the iron pot. José Genoino was still lying there. He seemed to have passed out, but was only resting after the thrashing that left him with bruises on his sides, legs, and stomach.

Two things were worrying Carlos Marra: what had happened to the helicopter he had requested to take them back to Xambioá, and how could he get the information he wanted out of the guerrillero? In answer to the first problem, there was nothing he could do but wait. As for the second, the best thing to do seemed to him to be to renew the torture. The sun was already going down over the jungle and the sky was turning red when he ordered his men to start beating the prisoner once more. Genoino could not believe everything was going to start all over again. Júlio turned his back so as not to see the beating, but he could hear the guerrillero's groans. It was not long before Marra had an idea that Júlio found even crueler than anything he had seen before. Following his orders, Ricardo took two empty sardine tins and put them on the ground, with the opened tops pointing upward. Tonho, Emanuel, and Forel made the young communist stand on them. Genoino could feel the sharp edges of the tins cutting into the soles of his feet. He clenched his teeth, and his eyes opened wide in pain. Forel grabbed him by the hair.

"Well, Geraldo? Are you going to talk?" asked Carlos Marra.

"I've told you, chief, I don't know anything," came the reply.

"Yes you do. I'm happy to stay here until you die from your suffering. If I were in your place, I'd have talked by now."

"But I've got nothing to say," said Genoino, between groans.

Time was going by and the prisoner wasn't giving them any information. Before it grew completely dark, Marra ordered Júlio to find something for the group to eat. Júlio was hungry, and thought it would be good to leave them and go hunting. But he suspected that when he got back he would find the young communist dead. His presence was unlikely to prevent such a tragedy, but he did not like the idea that he would not know what was going on in the hut. He thought the guerrillero was telling the truth when he said he knew nothing. It made no sense to kill him. But Júlio was not there to have an opinion: he had to follow Carlos Marra's orders. He picked up his rifle and went off to hunt for supper. The last rays of sunshine were struggling to pierce the canopy of trees. Despite all his experience hunting in the forest, Júlio imagined it would be difficult to find any target: by this time, many animals were already in their dens or sleeping in the treetops. He saw a sloth clinging to a branch and thought of shooting it. He did not like its meat but given the circumstances he could not afford the luxury of choice. But he thought better of it when he approached and saw the animal had a baby clinging to it.

He went on scanning the jungle until he spotted a spider

monkey about two feet long long lying on a bough fifty feet up. His bullet hit the animal straight in the head. The shot broke the silence of the forest and led to loud screeching from the macaws in the trees all around. Júlio picked the dead animal up from the ground and went back to the squad. During the almost thirty minutes he spent hunting, he couldn't stop thinking about what was happening in the hut. What kind of torture was the communist being subjected to now? Night had fallen by the time he reached the hut. Genoino was on the ground, hands still tied behind his back, and apparently unconscious. Carlos Marra and the others were resting seated around a fire that Emanuel had just lit.

Júlio approached them and threw the monkey on the ground near the fire. "There's our supper," he said. All of them had already eaten monkey, but none of them wanted to prepare the animal before roasting it. "After the fur and the skin are stripped off, it looks just like a baby. It's really horrible," said the chief. So Júlio had to perform that task as well. He walked down to a branch of the river about five hundred yards away and began the work. Plunging the monkey into the water, he used his knife to skin it, starting with the belly and ending with the head. It was only then that he realized Carlos Marra was right. Without skin or fur, the animal looked just like a newborn baby, mostly due to its pinkish skin and tiny arms and legs. He chopped its head and legs off, pulled out its innards, and then washed it with great care, scraping the carcass with his nails. He took advantage of being by the river to bathe and rest awhile. When he returned to the hut, he gave the monkey to Tonho, the group's cook. Cutting it into pieces, Tonho sprinkled them with salt and lime juice before throwing the pieces onto the fire to roast. The meat was tender, but they all complained Tonho had used too much salt. The dog smelled the food and came over. Marra threw him a big piece of flesh.

"Shall we give the communist some meat, chief?" asked Ricardo, when they had all eaten their fill. His concern for the prisoner took Júlio by surprise.

"No way! Let that bastard go hungry. Who told him to become a bandit?" Carlos Marra responded.

"Can I have the rest then?" asked Ricardo, revealing his true intentions.

"No, Ricardo. We're going to leave it for tomorrow. We're staying here until the army helicopter arrives, and I don't know when that will be. It could be tomorrow, but it could also take two or three days. My foot is really hurting. I'm in no mood to start walking through the jungle again."

Júlio listened carefully to all this and could only think that he would prefer to spend a week walking through the jungle than five minutes in a helicopter or anything else that left the ground. After they had eaten, the men stayed around the fire, talking about the usual topics: the guerrilla, women, and soccer. Carlos Marra, Forel, Tonho, Ricardo, and Emanuel recounted their adventures in "Vietnam," the name of the dirt street in Xambioá where the brothels were housed. It was called that because fights were always breaking out there. Invariably, the arguments centered around sex, alcohol, or money. In the worst cases, when people were killed, it was due to a combination of all three. As Júlio listened to the others boasting of their sexual adventures with the whores on Vietnam Street, he could not help but remember Ritinha. He was even tempted to tell them how wonderful it had been to have sex with her a week before he came to Araguaia, but then thought better of mentioning his sweetheart.

While the group was talking, the men went to bathe in the river one by one. Around eight in the evening, they put up the hammocks they were going to sleep in. At that moment, Carlos Marra, who had been sitting by the fire, got up and limped to the hut. He had recently come back from the river and had no shirt on, which made his belly seem even bigger. He sat on a wooden bench and, folding his arms across his stomach, told the men it was too early to go to sleep. Before they did, they would have to torture the prisoner again. None of them liked the idea: they were too tired to start punching and kicking him once more. They also agreed among themselves that the young guerrillero really did not know where the other rebel bases were. And if he did, he was not going to tell them.

"Chief, we're fed up with thumping this sonofabitch. We've beaten him black and blue, but he hasn't said a word," Emanuel said.

"I know. But I don't want you to punch him," Marra said.

"What then?" asked Ricardo.

"Take some sticks from the fire and burn the bastard's legs with them until he does talk. He'll be blabbing within the hour."

Júlio found it hard to reconcile the chief's soft, slow way of talking with such a cruel idea. But the others seemed to like what they heard. All of them, including Júlio, went over to the fire and each took out a burning stick, carefully holding them by the part not yet alight. The other ends were glowing brightly. José Genoíno was still lying curled up on the ground with his eyes closed, although he was awake. It had been almost fourteen hours since he was captured. For most of that time he had been punched and kicked. He had not eaten or drunk anything. He was so emotionally drained that he had not even managed to doze off. Júlio rushed over to him before the rest arrived.

"Tell us everything you know. You're going to die from all this punishment," Júlio said.

"But I don't know anything. I'm not lying," replied the guerrillero, his eyes still tight shut.

JOSÉ GENOINO NEVER forgot that brief exchange. He was confused when he saw this concern from the person he thought was the youngest in the group that had captured him. Faced with all the suffering and pain, he was pleased to find that at least one of his torturers was worried about his condition. This thought was still in his mind when he felt a vicious kick in his back. Opening his eyes, he saw six men standing around him. He realized he was going to face torture once more. When he saw they were holding burning sticks that lit up the darkness of the forest, he knew he would suffer even more than from another beating.

"Three of you hold him, and the other two burn his legs," Marra ordered.

Júlio was the first to throw away his stick. He preferred to hold the communist down than to burn him. Tonho and Forel did the same. When they bent down to grab hold of the guerrillero, they smelled a strong smell of urine. Unable to go into the forest to relieve himself, Genoino had wet himself. Ricardo and Emanuel pulled up his trousers and began the torture. Genoino felt the hot embers scorching his calves. He was shouting and writhing in pain. To make him suffer even more, Ricardo and Emanuel pressed the sticks hard against his legs and kept them there until his skin was red and raw. The young communist kicked out in agony, but he was held down by Júlio, Tonho, and Forel. Even today, José Genoino still bears the scars from those burns.

Carlos Marra watched all this still sitting on the ground.

"Well then, Geraldo? Are you going to tell us where your friends are hiding, or do you prefer to go on suffering?" he asked.

"I don't know anything. I've already told you a thousand times: I don't know a thing," Genoino shouted back.

Júlio glanced at the chief in the hope that he would order them to stop the torture. But he told them to go on burning Genoino's legs and went himself to fetch more sticks from the fire. Júlio was puzzled by the satisfied look he saw on the chief's face when the communist howled in pain. To this seventeen-year-old boy, however great the problem the guerrillero was causing the army, nothing justified so much cruelty. He was greatly relieved when finally Marra ordered them to tie their prisoner to a tree. "We have to sleep," said the chief, then instructed the five of them to sleep in turns so that someone was always keeping an eye on Genoino. Júlio, Tonho, Forel, Emanuel, and Ricardo decided among themselves the order of who should keep watch. Emanuel was the first, and Júlio the last. Marra was not included. Before they went to sleep, they dragged the unconscious guerrillero to a tree some ten yards from the hut. They tied him with his hands behind his back around the tree trunk. It was almost nine by the time all of them, except for Emanuel, went to sleep in the hut. The night passed without incident.

On the morning of April 17, they woke up around seven. It was already stiflingly hot. Júlio, who was the last man on guard duty, had already been up for two hours. He'd spent the whole time lying in his hammock outside with his eyes fixed on the prisoner, who seemed to be asleep. But Genoino, aching all over his body and with his burned legs, had not slept at all, simply rested. Marra and his men ate the monkey meat left over from the previous night and went back inside the hut, where they began talking again. Marra complained about how his foot was aching and cursed the fact that there was no sign of the helicopter. Emanuel suggested that two or three of them go down to the river to try to catch something for lunch and supper in case they had to spend another night there.

"If you like, I can go and fish, sir. I'm very good at it," said Júlio.

"We'll wait a little longer. If the army doesn't appear by midday, that's what we'll do," said Marra.

When the police chief's watch—the only one in the squad—showed exactly midday, he called Júlio and Tonho. He sent Tonho to relight the fire to cook lunch, and told Júlio not to come back from the river until he'd caught at least two pounds of fish. Tonho went to find sticks for the fire, while Júlio took his knife to chop off a branch to use as a harpoon for fishing. He was in the middle of sharpening the end of the branch when he heard a deafening noise above the trees. He looked up, but could not see anything, although he could imagine what that roar meant. The army helicopter landed in a flurry of leaves and dust. Carlos Marra leapt up from the bench and hobbled over to greet the officers. Júlio was worried. He'd decided to ask Marra to let him return to Xambioá by boat, but knew he would have to abide by whatever the chief decided. And Genoino had no idea if the arrival of the army meant things would be better or even worse for him. They could take him back to the town and free him right away. But they could also have already discovered that he was a militant in the Brazilian Communist Party and make his life even more wretched.

Carlos Marra was talking to the soldiers close to the helicopter, but Júlio couldn't hear what they were saying. From the stern expressions on the faces of the five men who were wearing green pants and shirts and black boots covered in dust, he guessed they were all very agitated. One of them climbed back into the helicopter and reappeared carrying an enormous drum. Marra ordered Ricardo to accompany the solider with the drum down to the river. They came back soon afterward, carrying the drum overflowing with water. The soldiers went over to Genoino. Only Marra and Ricardo from the group also approached the prisoner. Júlio, Tonho—who had returned from the forest—Forel, and Emanuel looked on from a distance.

"Let's see if he still refuses to talk," said the man apparently in command of the soldiers, staring into the eyes of Genoino, who was listening to everything fearfully. They untied him from the tree, but then bound his hands behind his back again. Two men seized his arms and plunged his head into the drum filled with water.

It was the worst thing José Genoino had ever experienced. With water up to his chest and unable to breathe, he gave a silent shout. He was swallowing the muddy river water and trying to lift his head out of the drum. Two hands forced him back down. Then all of a sudden someone yanked his head back. He spat out water and gulped down air. It felt as if his lungs were about to explode. Grabbing the back of his neck, one of the soldiers shouted: "Where are the other communists? Are you going to talk now or do you want to drown?" The answer was the same as he had given over and over to Carlos Marra: "I don't know any-thing." Genoino's head was plunged back underwater. With his eyes tight shut, he could feel a hand pushing his head one way and the other, his head banging against the aluminum sides. He lost count of how many times the process was repeated.

At the last one, he was sure he was going to die. He could not think of anything, apart from an overwhelming urge to live. He thrashed about in a desperate attempt to get some oxygen. His whole body was shaking in spasms that scared Júlio, who was watching everything from ten yards away. He pleaded with God to free Genoino from this agony. He thought his prayers had been answered when he saw one of the soldiers pull Genoino's head out of the water. The communist fell to the ground, water pouring from his mouth and coughing incessantly. The trauma from this torture was so great that for the next ten years Genoino was too afraid to bathe in rivers or the sea. "Let's go. We can continue the interrogation in town," shouted the man who seemed to be in command.

Carlos Marra glanced at his men and pointed toward the helicopter without a word. They all understood, and headed for the machine. Before embarking, the soldiers handcuffed the young communist and shackled his feet with a metal chain. They forced him to sit on the ground and took a photograph that was to become one of the most famous images of the Araguaia guerrilla. The atmosphere was so tense that Júlio decided not to ask Marra if he would allow him to return to Xambioá by boat. Saying one last prayer, he climbed into the helicopter and crouched in a corner. Genoino was bundled in by two soldiers whom Júlio thought looked as young as he was. Before they took off, he saw Ricardo helping two other soldiers set fire to the hut and everything in it. He also saw the dog running away from the fire toward the river. As the helicopter rose into the air, Júlio brought his knees up to his chest, clasped them in both hands, and closed his eyes tight. He only opened them again when they were back on the ground. José Genoino still had time to see the flames devouring the hut that had been the base for his guerrilla comrades.

Ten minutes later and they were back in Xambioá. Júlio was impressed by the speed with which they had reached the town. However dangerous it looked, the helicopter really was very swift and practical. When he heard Ricardo and Emanuel commenting how beautiful the rainforest was seen from above, he regretted not having been brave enough to open his eyes during the journey.

It was past two in the afternoon by the time Carlos Marra, all his group, José Genoino, and two soldiers reached the police jail in Xambioá. There followed three more days of interrogations and torture, but the prisoner went on denying being a guerrillero and claimed he knew nothing about what they were asking. Combining the evidence found in the forest and the testimonies of several inhabitants of the region who declared that Genoino was part of the armed movement, the army decided to send the alleged guerrillero—whose identity was still a secret—to the federal capital of Brasília, where he would be held by the Criminal Investigation Squad.

The transfer took place on April 22, 1972, in a Búfalo military transport plane. In the federal capital, José Genoino's identity was confirmed. He was in fact a member of the Communist Party of Brazil and had even been to prison before. This was in October 1968 in the town of Ibiúna near São Paulo, as a result of his political activity. The army soon came to the conclusion that he was one of the leaders of the Araguaia guerrilla.

A month later, he was taken back to Xambioá, where he was kept prisoner in the Army base set up on the town's soccer field. After two weeks of further torture—mostly beatings and electric shocks—and more interrogation, he was sent back to Brasília.

There he was kept in jail until in January 1973 he was sent to a military prison in São Paulo. He was only released on April 18, 1977, exactly five years to the day from the moment he had been wounded by a bullet from Júlio Santana's rifle in the rainforests of Araguaia. After his release, José Genoino returned to his life as a history professor. Five years later, he was elected as a federal deputy for the Workers' Party in São Paulo, with 58,000 votes. In 1998 he was reelected to the same position, this time winning 300,000 votes. This meant the ex-guerillero won the record for the most votes cast nationally in the lower chamber that year. It was only when he saw a report on TV about Genoino's electoral success where they showed the photo of him being captured in Araguaia that Júlio realized the man he shot in April 1972 had become an influential Brazilian politician.

The Second Death

BACK IN XAMBIOÁ in 1972, Júlio could not get to sleep. The boardinghouse bed, into which his five-foot-nine-tall body only just fitted, seemed to him even narrower and more uncomfortable. He could not get the scene he had witnessed that afternoon out of his mind. Shortly after lunch, soldiers and paratroopers from the Brazilian air force had hung the body of a skinny young man with dark hair and torn clothes head down from the branch of a tree close to the military camp set up on the Xambioá soccer field. The head was hanging only a couple of feet from the ground. A group of ten or twelve military personnel were mocking and insulting the dead man, kicking his face and neck. The body was swaying like a sack. Their kicks had already opened wounds on the man's face. His left eye was so swollen it looked like a red ball. Passersby in the street looked on fearfully. Neither Júlio nor any of the locals knew who this poor victim was, but thought he must be a guerrillero. And they were right. As Júlio later learned thanks to Carlos Marra, the body was that of Bergson Farias, a twenty-four-year-old from the state of Ceará. A Brazilian Communist Party militant, Bergson had been captured and killed that same morning (Monday, May 8, 1972) by members of the Brazilian air force in the Araguaia rainforest.

IT WAS THE disfigured body of this young communist that Júlio was struggling to forget so that he could get an undisturbed night's sleep. In vain. In the early hours he woke up several times breathing heavily and his body covered in sweat, less because of the fierce heat in Xambioá than due to the nightmares he had about Bergson's body swinging from the tree. All this violence was too much for him. He could not bear to see any more scenes like the torture of José Genoino or the body of Bergson Farias being kicked in full view of anyone passing by in the street. He wanted to go home. He wanted to return to the quiet life of the village where he lived on the banks of the river Tocantins in Porto Franco. Above all, he wanted to return to Ritinha's arms. The memory of her broad smile and always radiant look helped get him back to sleep.

It was already a little over a fortnight since Júlio had returned from the last operation in the rainforest when they had captured José Genoino. He was still sleeping in the boardinghouse. The good work he had done in the forest led police chief Marra to continue to pay for his lodgings. The town of Xambioá was in turmoil. Due to the military personnel who kept on arriving (it is estimated that during the Araguaia Guerrilla, almost four thousand troops were brought into the region), there was a shortage of everything. Food, drink, cigarettes, toiletries. All the best items in the town's small markets were snapped up by members of the army, navy and air force. The three thousand or more local inhabitants had to make do with what was left.

In Xambioá, Júlio was constantly called on to work for the army. Among the tasks he was given, he least liked having to chop down trees to enlarge the area of the military camp and to create a landing strip for the Air force planes. His hands were already callused from spending hours wielding the ax. He also occasionally helped build the wooden huts that were to serve as clinics, lodging and sleeping quarters for the soldiers. However much he disliked this kind of job, he preferred to be there, in the town, than in the forest tracking down communists. The last thing he wanted in life was to shoot another man. In those days this was all that was talked about in Xambioá, apart from the episode of the guerrillero hanging from the tree—his body was only removed in the early hours of the following day when vultures were already starting to feed on the corpse.

This event had created a climate of fear in the population. Everyone was terrified at the cruelty shown by the military, which was precisely what the commanders of the operation intended, as Carlos Marra explained to Júlio at the police station.

"They need to understand that this can happen to anyone who aids the communists," the chief told his men.

"What do you mean, chief? Does that mean they can kill people from the town simply because someone helps the communists?" asked Forel, whose family lived in Xambioá.

"Of course, my lad. Whoever helps the communists is acting against the people. And whoever is against the people will be treated as though they were a communist as well. That's the only way we're going to finish with this scum."

Júlio listened in silence, fearful of Carlos Marra's harsh words. He could tell that lots more terrible things were still going to happen in the region. That night, the police chief said he would pay for his men to "have some fun." That was the expression Marra used to refer to the street known as "Vietnam," Xambioá's red-light district. It was a street of beaten earth with about ten wooden shacks lit by red lamps, where the attraction was women in scanty clothing and heavy makeup. Júlio was the only one in the group who had not yet taken advantage of the services offered by "the Vietnam girls," as the prostitutes were called by their clients.

"There are all sorts of women there, Julão," said the police chief, trying to tempt the boy to visit the street.

"I really don't want to go, sir. Let me stay here, looking after the station," said Júlio, who was not yet eighteen.

"You say the same every time. Today that won't do. You'll have to go with us," Carlos Marra decreed.

This was the third or fourth time Marra had invited Júlio to visit "Vietnam." Until now, he had always refused and stayed in the police station. On this occasion, however, he took advantage of the chief's insistence to go and satisfy his curiosity about what went on in those houses whose doors were always open, but which were covered with brightly colored curtains. In the end he, Marra, Forel, and Emanuel went. The street was packed with men. The military personnel strutted along in their uniforms, which seemed to attract the attention of the "girls" who smiled and waved to them. In one of the doors, Júlio saw a girl with light skin and blond hair smiling at him. She was wearing a tight, very short skirt that showed her sturdy thighs, and a red bra. Carlos Marra noticed them exchange glances and asked whether the boy wanted to meet the girl. "No, chief. I only came here to see what it's like," Júlio replied, just as he saw Emanuel and Forel being dragged into another of the houses by two women he thought looked ugly and old. Looking back, he saw the girl with plump legs was still watching him with a smile on her face.

"You want that girl, don't you? Let's go there. You can have her," said Marra.

"No, sir. I don't want anything. Let's keep walking."

"No way. Let's go there right now," said the police chief, tugging at the boy's arm.

Without another word, Marra went into the shack where the girl was. Taking her by the hand, he ordered:

"Stay with my friend. Look after him right away, and I'll settle everything with you later."

"Of course, chief," the young girl replied.

Seeing Carlos Marra come in, a tall, rather stocky woman about five feet seven with blond hair under a headscarf came out from behind a counter covered in blue tiles. Júlio saw the chief greet her politely, bowing slightly to kiss her right hand. Another two women were chatting on a dark-colored sofa with the stuffing coming out.

The girl told to look after Júlio sat him down in an armchair and sat sideways on his lap. He did not know what to do, or where to put his hands.

"What's your name?" she asked.

"Júlio."

"Did you know you're very good-looking?" she went on, stroking his face and arms. He looked down and smiled, embarrassed.

The girl leaned forward until her face was touching his, and began caressing his chest. He felt he was doing something wrong, but was enjoying the way she was stroking him. He became aroused. Still sitting on his lap, she began to move her hips, and the smile did not leave her face. With one of her hands, the "girl" caressed his face, neck, and ears. With the other, she began to stroke him intimately. Júlio recalled when Ritinha had touched him in the same way. But with her it was different. Ritinha did not have a sly face like this one, nor red lipstick or those provocative clothes that seemed to be dancing in his lap. He could not understand why, but the impression he was doing something forbidden made him even more excited. The girl was rubbing herself so much against him that Júlio could see her panties. They were black, the same color as her skirt. He could not control himself any longer, and roughly pushed open her thighs.

"Let's go to the room," she said, taking him by the right hand. The boy glanced over at the police chief, who was still deep in conversation with the woman who appeared to own the place. Marra smiled at Júlio and gave a slight nod of the head, as if approving the girl's decision. The two of them walked toward the back of the house along a corridor no more than five feet wide, lined with doors made of planks. They went into the last one on the left. Everything was very dark, with only a yellow lamp lighting the room. The girl made him lie down on the bed, the only piece of furniture to be seen. Júlio smelled a dreadful stench. It was so awful he opened his eyes and raised his hand to his nose in disgust. Through the cracks in the planks he could hear noises and groans coming from the adjoining room. Stretching out on top of him, Cibele—as she said she was called—undid her bra. Without stirring, he watched as she removed his trousers and underpants in a single movement. He was nervous, unable to move, but still very excited.

"Are you a virgin?" she wanted to know.

"No," said the boy, but nothing more.

"Stay still."

The girl's body seemed to slide over his. She began to kiss his neck, then moved down to his chest, stomach, and finally down there. His uncle Cícero had told him to ask Ritinha to do this, but he had never had the courage. He never thought he could feel such pleasure. His whole body was shaking. Cibele sucked him hungrily. Thirstily. He still had his eyes closed. By now Júlio was panting. A shiver ran down his spine and he gave a deep moan. Cibele withdrew her mouth and pressed down on him with rapid up-and-down movements, until the boy almost fainted.

"Did you enjoy it, Júlio?" she asked, the same smile still on her face.

"You bet!" he replied, still panting and feeling weak. As he regained his strength, he saw Cibele pick her bra up from a corner of the room, straighten her hair, put on her sandals, and adjust her miniskirt. She handed him his trousers and under-pants. He dressed quickly, and they both went back to the main room.

"Already?" said Marra, who was still talking to the brothel owner.

"The boy is quick, chief," said Cibele.

"But you were in there for less than ten minutes. Was it good, Julão?" Marra continued.

The reply came with a vigorous nod of the head. Carlos Marra took a swig from his glass of beer and asked the owner how much it would be.

"The beer is on the house. The girl is ten cruzeiros," she said.

"That's too much. I'll pay five," said the police chief, taking a five-cruzeiro note from his pocket and laying it on the counter. The woman took the money without a word. Júlio was puzzled that Marra paid the same as it cost him to have lunch in Xambioá for those few minutes with Cibele. He had loved what the girl had done to him in that stinking room, but still thought the lunch was worth more. Marra wanted to take him to get to know other houses in the street, but he preferred to go back to the boardinghouse to sleep. Not without first asking God for forgiveness for lying with that kind of woman. He felt dirty. While Ritinha was probably at home awaiting his return, he had just had sex with a girl who charged for it. He could not deny that he had enjoyed, really enjoyed, what he experienced in the bed with Cibele. But he was determined he would not do anything like that again. And yet that night he fell asleep thinking he would like to have Cibele there in the bed beside him so that she could do all that over again.

In the days that followed, Júlio's routine never varied. He woke up early—always before seven o'clock, ate two buns with cheese and a Coca-Cola in the corner bakery, then went on to the police station where Carlos Marra would tell him what he had to do that day. Over the past three weeks, this had meant presenting himself at the military camp to help in whatever way they asked. On this particular morning, Carlos Marra told him that, in two or three days' time, they would be going out again on another operation tracking down guerrilleros in the jungles of Araguaia. He also said he had received a message from Júlio's uncle, Cícero Santana.

"He said he'll come to see you at the end of the month," said Marra.

"About time too. It's been a month more or less since I last saw my uncle," the boy replied.

On May 10, 1972, Júlio, Carlos Marra, Emanuel, and Forel left Xambioá for another foray into the rainforest. They spent six days combing the region in search of communists and warning the local population to collaborate with the army's work. They did not capture any members of the revolutionary movement, but the police chief declared himself content with the contacts they made with the locals. Marra stopped to talk with them at each house they came across on the way. He distributed clothing, tools, medicines, and at the same time threatened them that if they did not help the armed forces catch the guerrilleros they themselves would be arrested and tortured.

"I'm sure that if these people got to hear of any movements by the communists in this region, we would soon know about it," he said, when the group was heading back to Xambioá.

TWO DAYS AFTER their return to the town, Júlio was at the police station waiting for orders from Carlos Marra, when four soldiers came in with a prisoner, hands tied behind his back. It was the afternoon of Thursday, May 18, and the prisoner was the boatman Lourival Moura, a dark-complexioned man with black, curly hair aged around forty and five foot nine. One of the soldiers explained that he had been collaborating with the guerrilleros. The boatman said that was not true, that he had never helped any communist. He was silenced by a punch to the stomach.

"Throw this bastard into the cell, chief. We'll be back later to get him to talk," said the man who was apparently in command of the others.

"Of course, lieutenant. These people are all the same. They start by saying they've done nothing, but they soon spill the beans," replied Carlos Marra.

He told Júlio that from then on it was his responsibility to keep an eye on the prisoner. This meant he was to stay in the station when Marra and his men were not there—mainly at night. The lad would therefore have to sleep at the station. From Marra's conversation with the lieutenant, Júlio learned that Lourival had been arrested because he was accused of helping the guerrilleros, buying them supplies and ammunition, and even lending his boat for the transport of rebels. The boatman was thrown into an empty cell measuring thirteen by thirteen feet.

That same night, Júlio was on his own at the station when two men in army uniforms came to interrogate the prisoner. Marra had told him he was going to pay a visit to "Vietnam" and that he would be back later to see how things were going. Júlio handed the key to the cell to one of the soldiers and stood at the front door to the station. Within a few minutes he began to hear shouts that soon became increasingly terrifying. He thought perhaps he should go back in to see what was going on, but decided it would be best to stay where he was. It had nothing to do with him: his job was simply to remain in the building whenever Carlos Marra was not there.

Almost an hour later, the two soldiers gave him back the key and left.

"Tell the chief that tomorrow night we'll be back to carry on the interrogation," said one of them.

Júlio waited until the soldiers were out sight and went in to see how the prisoner was. He found Lourival on the floor of the cell, in his underpants, with cuts on his legs and bruises on his face. Hearing someone open the door, the boatman muttered:

"I've already told you, I know nothing. I didn't help anyone."

"What have they done to you?" asked Júlio.

"They said they would cut my whole body if I don't tell them where the people from São Paulo are hiding. But I don't know that, lad. I don't know."

News that the boatman was in jail quickly spread through Xambioá. Lourival Moura lived and worked in the region, and was known as a quiet man. The day after his arrest, four youngsters who worked with him went to the police station. They wanted to see how Moura was, but Marra refused to permit it. He said that only family members could see the prisoner. Less than an hour later, Lourival's son, a lanky fourteen-year-old, appeared in the doorway of the station. He had brought a hammock and a pot filled with rice, manioc flour, beans, and roast meat.

"What's that for?" asked the chief, without getting up from his seat.

"My mom got me to bring it for my dad," said the youth, eyes fixed on the ground.

"Leave it there, I'll make sure he gets it," said Marra, pointing to the desk.

"Mom said I should give it to my dad myself, to see how he is."

"Kid, your father is the worse for wear. It's nothing serious, but I can't let a boy like you go into his cell. Leave the things there on the desk and I'll have them sent in to your father right away," said the chief, motioning to Júlio to go and take the hammock and pan from the boy.

"But Mom said I was not to go home without talking to my dad," he insisted.

"That's not possible today. Tell your mother you'll be able to talk to your father. If she wants to come with you, I'll let both of you talk to him."

As the prisoner was in the station, Carlos Marra allowed Júlio to go back to sleep in the boardinghouse and sent for two soldiers to spend the night guarding Lourival.

On Saturday, May 20, Júlio woke up anxious to see how the prisoner was. He didn't know why, but he believed Lourival was telling the truth when he swore he had nothing to do with the guerrilla. In fact, he was wrong about this. As he was to learn later, the boatman did collaborate with the communists.

Júlio reached the station around seven thirty in the morning. Two soldiers were chatting while they waited for the arrival of Carlos Marra, who had promised he would be there by eight. They told Júlio the prisoner had spent a good night. He went to the cell, and saw Lourival curled up in a corner, covered by the hammock his son had left. He had apparently not been tortured again.

Shortly before lunchtime, the boatman's son and wife reached the station. The chief himself met them.

"You said we could come today to see my husband," the woman said.

"That's true, but I forgot today is Saturday. You'll have to forgive me, but visits to the station are only permitted from Monday to Friday."

"Sir, you yourself told my son we could come to talk to my husband today—"

"I know, and I'm very sorry. But you have to understand . . . it's the regulations. I can't let any visitor talk to prisoners at the weekend. Come back on Monday, and I promise that you and your son will be able to talk to Lourival."

"Can I leave this food I brought for him?"

"Of course. Leave it with me, and I'll make sure he gets it."

"We'll be back on Monday morning, okay?" said the boatman's wife as she left.

She never saw her husband alive again. That night, Carlos Marra and his men went to have fun with the women in "Vietnam." Júlio was relieved to have been chosen to stay in the station, guarding the prisoner: he still could not forgive himself for having betrayed Ritinha. He did not want to go with that kind of woman again, however pleasurable Cibele's caresses had been. On his own in the police station, he felt important. Seated in Marra's chair, he could hear Lourival groaning. He considered going to see how the prisoner was, but thought it wiser to obey Carlos Marra's orders: he had told him not to go to the cell "for any reason."

Around midnight, the police chief, Forel, and two soldiers arrived. They were all drunk. They were talking in loud voices, smiling exaggeratedly and reeking of rum.

"How is our friend, Julão?" asked Marra, slapping Júlio on the chest.

"He's in the cell, chief. Groaning all the time."

"Poor thing. He must be suffering a lot. We'll put an end to that as quickly as we can," said Marra, going toward the cell at the back of the building.

Forel and the two soldiers went with him. Júlio preferred to stay in the doorway to the station, praying nothing bad would happen. The street was deserted. No one apart from the occasional drunk coming back from "Vietnam." He heard Lourival cry out desperately. His cries were so loud that one of the passersby looked toward the station with a horrified expression on his face. Júlio did not know what to do. He was curious to see what was going on in the cell, but at the same time was sure he would not like what he saw one little bit. He did not want to witness any more torture. If he could not help the poor prisoner, better to leave at once.

"Chief, can I go and sleep at the boardinghouse?" he shouted, leaning on the doorframe.

"What's that?" Marra shouted back.

Júlio walked to the partition separating the main room from the cell and repeated what he had said. Lourival's cries sounded even more disturbing.

"I'm very tired and dying of sleep. You know I always wake up early. Can I go back to the boardinghouse to sleep?" he said.

"Fine. But tomorrow I want you here by eight."

"Okay. I'm going now. See you tomorrow."

"See you. Close the front door and throw the key near the desk."

That night, Júlio was so worried he could not close his eyes. He tossed and turned in the bed, sat up, got up. He was so upset that he left his room before daybreak and went to the back of the boardinghouse. He sat on a wooden crate lying in the midst of the pigs and chickens that the landlady kept. He could not get Lourival's cries of pain out of his head. He was ashamed of not having tried to intervene to help the boatman. He knew his opinion wouldn't make the slightest difference to the chief, but at least he would not have been such a coward. His throat was dry, and so on his way to his room he turned on the faucet about two feet off the ground on the muddy wall. He knelt and drank water until he was no longer thirsty. He went back to bed, and was lying there when he saw the first light of day filtering in through the cracks in the wooden door. It must have been around six on Sunday, May 21.

Carlos Marra had said he should only appear at the station at eight o'clock, but Júlio did not want to wait that long. He remained stretched out on his bed for what he thought were another thirty or forty minutes, then got up. He put on his trousers and shirt, and washed his face at the same faucet. He did not even stop at the bakery where he usually had his breakfast, simply asking the man who served him what time it was. Ten past seven. When he got to the police station, he found the door locked. Going around the back, he tried the rear door. It was also shut. He returned to the front and hammered on the wood.

"Who is it?" asked a man who from his voice sounded like Forel.

"It's me, Forel. Julão."

Forel opened the door just enough to spot the youngster and give him a five-cruzeiro bill.

"Go to the bakery and spend this on bread, cheese, and butter. And bring a pot of coffee. Tell them it's for the chief," said Forel.

"Can I buy myself a Coca-Cola?" Júlio asked.

"Of course, kid."

"Okay," Júlio replied, and ran off.

He was back again in less than ten minutes. He put the bag with what he'd bought on the chief's desk and went quickly and nervously down to the cell. Lourival's body was hanging two feet from the ground, tied upside down by the chest to a wooden beam, wearing only his underpants. His bulging eyes looked as if they had been painted red. There was a purple swelling the size of an orange on the left side of the boatman's face. There were long red stripes on his stomach, which Júlio guessed had been made by him being beaten with the end of the broom he could see thrown into a corner of the cell. Frowning, Júlio's mouth dropped open in horror when he saw several cuts on Lourival's legs. Some of them were still bleeding. The dead man's hands were tied behind his back. Júlio considered taking the body down from this improvised gibbet, but thought it best to do nothing. He went back to the main room. Forel was eating French bread with cheese and butter. He had a glass of coffee in his left hand.

"What happened here, Forel?" Júlio wanted to know.

"What do you mean?"

"The prisoner is dead back there in the cell. Were you the ones who did that to him? Was it the chief who had the poor guy killed?"

"I don't know anything, Julão," Forel said, taking another bite of bread.

Júlio made himself a sandwich, with plenty of butter and a generous slice of cheese. He opened the bottle of Coca-Cola by putting the top on the edge of the desk and hitting it as hard as he could. He had learned to open bottles like that with his uncle Cícero. Forel was eating his second bread stick when Carlos Marra and Emanuel arrived. Seeing the chief come in, Forel and Júlio stood up, both of them holding their sandwiches.

"It's great you've already bought food," Marra said. "Emanuel and I are dying of hunger. We've been with the military until now."

Emanuel prepared sandwiches for himself and the chief.

"How is our friend back there in the cell?" Marra asked Forel.

"Still there, chief. Just like before."

Carlos Marra sat down in his chair, took a swig of coffee, and began to eat the bread and cheese. Júlio really wanted to ask who had done that to Lourival, but was afraid he would be reprimanded. He was standing silently in a corner of the room drinking his Coca-Cola when Marra seemed to guess what he was feeling and thinking.

"Are you nervous, Julão?" he asked, in that deep but calm voice of his.

"No, I'm not."

"You're very quiet. You haven't said a word since I arrived. What's the matter?"

"Nothing, chief."

"Spit it out, kid!" ordered Marra, raising his voice a little.

Júlio decided to tell him what was worrying him.

"Chief, when I left here last night, the prisoner was alive. When I arrived this morning, I found he was dead," said the boy.

"What of it?" Marra replied.

"Nothing. I only wanted to know how he died."

"He killed himself, Julão. He was so afraid of going to jail for having helped the communists that he decided to kill himself."

Júlio knew Carlos Marra was lying, but he did not want to annoy the chief any further with his questions, so he pretended to believe the version that the boatman had committed suicide. Shortly after Marra arrived, Lourival's wife and son entered the police station. The boy was carrying a pot wrapped in a stained cloth. The wife was a sturdy woman just over five feet tall, with a round face, thin lips, and small eyes. She was wearing a head-scarf. When he saw her and the boy come in, Júlio quickly left the station, eyes on the ground. From outside, he heard Lourival's wife saying she wanted to see her husband and would not wait a day longer. Marra said a tragedy had occurred: Lourival had committed suicide. Júlio heard his widow shout desperately: "You killed my husband! Murderers! Murderers!"

Without raising his voice, Carlos Marra took her to task, saying she could be arrested for contempt of authority but that he would not do so simply because of the pain she must be suffering. Júlio was glad he was outside the station: he could not bear to be called an assassin by the boatman's wife. She was insisting that she wanted to see her husband's body. Marra said that was impossible. "Only after we have carried out the autopsy," he explained. Sitting on the ground in the street, Júlio could hear everything. He knew why Marra did not want to allow the dead man's family to visit the cell. Anyone who saw that smashed body, hanging head down and with his hands tied behind his back, would realize he had been murdered. After arguing with Marra for ten minutes, Lourival's wife and son left the station. The widow was sobbing and howling as she clutched her son, who was about six inches taller than her.

News of Lourival's death spread through Xambioá. Everyone said that the boatman had been killed by Carlos Marra and his men, but the police chief didn't seem to care what was being rumored. On the contrary. That night he sent Forel to "Vietnam" to tell people that, yes, Lourival had been killed by the army with great cruelty. To demonstrate how ruthless he and his friends could be, Forel described Lourival's death in great detail. He told them for example that before the boatman was finished off they had used a pair of pliers to tear out all his fingernails—something that Júlio had not seen. Forel said that the same treatment and the same death awaited all those who collaborated with the guerrilleros or simply withheld information that could help the military capture them. The official version about Lourival's death that Marra announced publicly was different. According to him, he had committed suicide. The motive: fear of being sent to jail for having helped the communists. "Lourival kept on saying that he preferred to die rather than be sent to prison," Marra said.

Júlio spent the whole night thinking about the boatman's death. How could the police chief, Forel, and Emanuel be so cruel and violent? The men with whom he had become accustomed to spend day after day tracking through the jungle, talking, eating, and sleeping together, were not only capable of killing someone but, even worse, did not show the slightest remorse. He had already felt the weight of taking a person's life, and although that had been nine months earlier, he was sure his sense of guilt for that crime would never stop troubling his soul. That night, before he fell asleep, he asked God to deliver him from this hell. He was exhausted from seeing so much horror and violence. He wanted to go back to the peace and quiet of his village in Porto Franco on the banks of the river Tocantins. When he prayed like this, he could never have imagined he was only three weeks away from committing his second killing.

MARIA LÚCIA PETIT DA SILVA was a twenty-two-year-old woman, five foot four and weighing around 100 pounds. She had shoulder-length auburn hair, an aquiline nose, and dark eyes with a slight squint. Trained as a teacher, she worked in a primary school, the Escola Aviador Frederico Gustavo dos Santos, in São Paulo. Toward the end of 1969 she joined the Communist Party of Brazil. Her family and friends said her greatest dream was to help educate the children of Brazil's poor interior. At first working as a volunteer, she was soon chosen to go to Goiás state. She was happy: this was exactly what she wanted. In January 1970, she went to the south of Pará state, and then moved to help with the guerrilla's social work in the Araguaia region. She spent most of her time teaching children to read and write, and explaining to young people and adults what the guerrilla was fighting for. She always claimed that the struggle was for social equality in Brazil. She often said it was unacceptable to live in a country where a few had so much and so many had so little. Her lessons and speeches were full of affection; she was always good-humored and very close to the children of the region. In this way she won the friendship and respect of all the towns in Araguaia where she worked. She was frequently asked to be the godmother of newly born babies.

A few days before she died, she had received one such invitation. A farmer known as João Cocoió had asked her to attend the baptism of his two-month-old son. She accepted, not suspecting that this same man would betray her to the army.

This was in early June 1972. The military was putting the inhabitants of the Araguaia region under all kinds of pressure to help them capture communists. Violence was one of the means most frequently used by the army to force the local inhabitants to denounce the presence of guerrilleros. The soldiers killed their animals—horses, oxen, and chickens—beat up whoever they felt like, and even burned the farmers' crops and houses.

João Cocoió, a man of around forty, married and the father of three children—including the newborn baby María Lúcia was to be godmother to—had already received this kind of warning from the army when his manioc plantation was set on fire by half a dozen soldiers. He was afraid of placing his family in danger, and so that the army would leave them in peace, he decided to betray the presence of the group of which Maria Lúcia was a part in the region known as Pau Preto, in the south of Pará.

As they could not appear in the towns for fear of being identified and arrested, the guerrilleros usually asked local inhabitants to buy supplies, tobacco, and ammunition for the rebel movement. João Cocoió had been given the task of going to Xambioá to bring cigarettes, beans, rice, coffee, and ammunition for the communists. When he reached town, before he even bought these supplies, he went straight to the police station and told

Carlos Marra everything. Standing in a corner of the station, Júlio overheard the conversation between Cocoió and Marra. The peasant farmer spoke for no more than ten minutes. He did not have the information the chief considered most important: the exact location of the revolutionary camp. But Carlos Marra shifted in his wooden chair and bent forward, elbows on the desk, when he heard Cocoió say he knew where three of the guerrilleros would be on the morning of June 16.

"I came to town to buy some things they wanted. We agreed they would pick them up at my house early on Friday," said Cocoió, who was sitting opposite the police chief, shuffling his feet nervously.

"Who are the three?" asked Marra.

"Cazuza, Mundico, and Maria."

Cazuza was the alias of Miguel Pereira, from Pernambuco. Aged twenty-nine, he died in Araguaia in September 1972. Mundico was Rosalindo Souza from Bahia, aged thirty-three. He was killed a year later, still fighting with the guerrilla. Maria Lúcia, Cazuza, and Mundico belonged to the detachment of guerrilleros whose base was in the region of Pau Preto, about two miles from João Cocoió's house.

"Good," said Carlos Marra. "Go and do what they asked of you here. Act as if I knew nothing about it. Don't change anything you agreed with the communists."

"Of course, chief."

"If we succeed in capturing those three, I promise you will be well rewarded."

When the farmer left the station, Marra signaled with his right hand for Júlio to come over to the desk.

"Follow that guy, Julão. I want to know everything he does in town."

"Yes sir," the boy replied.

"Julão, be careful. I need to know everything that man does here. Everything. If he stops to spit, I want you to tell me. Understood?"

"Understood, chief. Don't worry. But let me leave now, before he disappears," said Júlio, rushing out of the station just in time to see Cocoió turn the corner. The task proved much easier than Júlio had expected. First the famer went into a grocery store. Júlio watched from a distance through the piles of goods on wooden shelves. He saw the man leave carrying a sack containing beans, rice, coffee, and five or six packs of cigarettes. From there, Cocoió headed for one of the two stores that sold guns in Xambioá. It was in a small kiosk that measured at most eighty-six square feet. There were no corridors or shelves that could help hide Júlio from the man he was following. It was little more than a counter, behind which a white-haired old man—who Júlio calculated must be as old as his father's father—served the customers. The weapons and ammunition of all kinds were kept in cabinets behind the counter. No one could get to that side. Júlio sat on the bare earth that was scorching from the heat of the sun, taking cover behind an army jeep parked some five yards from the gun store.

He followed Cocoió until he left town and disappeared into the forest on a brown horse. Less than ten minutes later, Júlio was back at the gun store. From a quick conversation with the white-haired old man, he learned that the farmer had bought two boxes of bullets for a .12 rifle and three boxes for a .38 revolver. He went back to the police station feeling proud of himself. He was sure he'd done a good job. He even knew that Cocoió had stopped at Alberto's bar and ordered a beer, but had not drunk the whole bottle, only two glassfuls, and then left. He was sure Carlos Marra would congratulate him on a job well done. And so he did.

"Very good, Julão. You're getting better and better at this," the chief said after the youngster had given him a detailed report.

THREE DAYS LATER, after almost four hours' march through the forest, Júlio, Carlos Marra, and three soldiers arrived at João Cocoió's house. Forel had also been chosen by the police chief to join the operation led by the army, but he had contracted leishmaniasis and was in bed with leg ulcers and a high fever.

Cocoió's house was made of wood with a palm roof. There was no furniture apart from five benches the farmer himself had made, five hammocks, and a fire. His wife and children weren't there: aware there was a strong possibility there would be a clash and a shoot-out between the soldiers and the communists, Cocoió had sent his family to his mother-in-law's in Pau Preto. That night, while they were all eating rice with roast chicken, Cocoió asked if they would allow him to leave: he did not want to see them capture the guerrilleros. The man apparently in command of the soldiers saw no problem with that, but Carlos Marra insisted he stay.

"Be a man, Cocoió," he told him, sitting on one of the benches with his plate on his knees and his belly hanging out.

"I am a man, chief. It's just that I don't want to be here when all hell breaks loose," Cocoió replied.

"Well then, you've left it too late. Hell began here a long time ago," said Marra, his mouth full of rice. He went on:

"And don't even think of disappearing in the early hours, do you hear me? We might need you here tomorrow morning."

On the morning of Friday, June 16, 1972, Júlio was awakened by Carlos Marra pushing the hammock he was sleeping in. When he opened his eyes he saw it was still dark. The chief wanted them all up and on their feet as early as possible. By the time the first rays of the sun began to light up the forest, Júlio, Marra, the three soldiers, and Cocoió were sitting on a log outside the house. Apart from the farmer, they were all armed. The soldiers had 7.62mm assault rifles that were used exclusively by the army and which Júlio had never seen before. But he was happy with his own weapon. Carlos Marra had his .38 revolver tucked into his waistband. He always kept it with him, even when he went to have fun in "Vietnam."

The plan was to capture the three communists alive when they came to Cocoió's house to pick up the goods he'd bought for them in Xambioá. Júlio was pleased he would not have to kill anyone, yet at the same time was worried he would have to witness more torture as he had when José Genoino had been caught two months earlier.

The group lay in wait for the guerrilleros in the midst of dense jungle. In their dark green uniforms, the soldiers seemed to merge with the undergrowth. Júlio was still hoping he could get clothes like that. Especially the boots. He was admiring the thick, long-sleeved shirt of the soldier beside him when he saw three people walking toward them about forty yards away. He threw a stick at Carlos Marra, who was five yards to his right, and pointed in the direction of the communists. The police chief had made it very clear: if there was an exchange of gunfire, the first shots had to come from the soldiers. Only after that could Júlio fire. As a precaution, the lad trained his rifle on one of the guerrilleros. He was starting to enjoy this kind of job. It gave him a strange feeling of power to know that someone's life was in his hands. All he had to do was pull the trigger, and the poor guy would be dead. But he would not do that: he had promised God he would never kill anyone again.

His thoughts were abruptly interrupted by a series of explosions that terrified him. Shots from 7.62 rifles tore through the undergrowth, the sound echoing all over the forest. Júlio saw the three guerrilleros start to run back into the trees, away from Cocoió's house. He noticed that the smallest of the three communists had been wounded and was escaping with difficulty, trailing one leg. The other two, who were slightly ahead, came back to help their injured comrade. The soldiers carried on shooting. The trees, some of them almost ten feet in diameter, helped protect the rebels from the bullets. The two unharmed guerrilleros started firing at the soldiers. One of them put his arm around the injured rebel to help, in a desperate attempt to escape. The other rebel went on firing his revolver.

Júlio was in a panic. He had never felt his heart beat so wildly. He felt certain that at any moment one of the bullets could hit him. This was the first time he had been in a shoot-out of this kind. Marra looked across at him and shouted something he couldn't hear properly above the gunfire. The chief repeated, louder still: "Bring one of them down. At least one of them."

Without knowing why, Júlio thought it would be better to shoot the communist who had already been wounded. Kneeling down on the leaf-strewn earth, he took up the position he always adopted when he had to shoot. He put his left knee on the ground and rested his right elbow on the other leg. Closing his left eye, he took aim at the right shoulder of the wounded guerrillero. He remembered the day he had shot José Genoino. The scene was identical: the undergrowth blocking a good view, the rebel trying to escape, his own heart racing, his breath coming in short gasps. The pressure of making sure he did not miss. He enjoyed that. He waited for the precise moment and pulled the trigger. Even before the bullet hit the target, he saw there would be a disaster. Because of the leg wound, the injured communist leaned slightly to the right and bent his knees. These movements meant that the shot aimed at the shoulder in fact hit the left side of the rebel's head. The body fell to the ground and lay without moving. Júlio realized what had happened, but hoped against hope he had not just killed another person. All the pain and confusion he'd felt on the day he murdered Amarelo came back to torment his soul. He soon realized, though, that there was no need to go any closer: he knew he had killed the guerrillero. He was sure of it. And so right there, in the midst of the rainforest, he began to pray the ten Hail Marys and twenty Our Fathers that he believed would bring him a divine pardon. He saw the other two rebels running away desperately. Marra and the three soldiers went up to the body sprawled in the undergrowth. Júlio stayed where he was, kneeling down, throwing away the rifle with a strength he didn't know he possessed, and praying with an equally unsuspected fervor.

He was still praying when he heard Marra calling him. Against his will, he went over to where the body had fallen. The ground beneath the corpse's head was drenched with blood. As he approached, he heard one of the soldiers say: "It's a woman." Júlio felt even guiltier. For reasons he himself could not explain, he thought that killing a woman was worse than taking a man's life. The dead guerrillero's face looked serene. Her eyes were still open. Her clean-cut features and short shoulder-length hair made her look even younger than her twenty-two years. She was wearing dark gray canvas trousers, and a blue long-sleeved shirt.

"You shouldn't have killed her, Julão. I told you not to kill her," Carlos Marra said in a solemn but quiet voice.

"I know, chief. I didn't intend to kill anyone, but when I fired, she moved to one side and the bullet hit her in the head."

"It's not a problem," said one of the soldiers whom Marra called "lieutenant." "It could even be a good thing, to show these communists we're not here to play games. Either they give up their idea of revolution, or they'll die one by one."

Júlio was scared of this man and his harsh words. Carlos Marra ordered him and another soldier to carry the body to Cocoió's house. Júlio took the guerrillera by the ankles, the other lad grabbed her by the wrists. A stab of pain ran through Júlio as he touched the young woman's body. Her eyes were still wide open and it was as if she were staring at him, condemning him for what he had just done.

At that moment, Júlio recalled the day he had killed Amarelo, in August 1971. On that occasion, his victim's eyes had also stayed open after death. Now he felt very strange having to carry the lifeless body. His hands broke into a cold sweat. He had never spent so long with a corpse. He felt like vomiting. He wanted to be free of the body as quickly as possible. It was almost three hundred yards' walk from the forest to Cocoió's house.

After that, two of the soldiers stayed with the dead guerrillera, while Marra, Júlio, and the lieutenant returned to Xambioá.

They reached town at around two in the afternoon, and went straight to the army base. From there the lieutenant sent a helicopter to fetch the two soldiers and the body. During the whole trek back to Xambioá, Júlio stayed silent. His heart was heavy, and he felt the same nausea and unease he'd experienced the day he had killed Amarelo. He even refused the rice and jerked meat they'd brought from Cocoió's house to eat on the way back to town.

As soon as the helicopter took off, Carlos Marra and Júlio headed for the police station. When they arrived, he heard the chief say he understood why the youngster was so silent and downcast. No one could be happy at having killed a woman. But that was part of their job. Their mission was to wipe out the guerrilla, and Júlio was showing he was an increasingly important part of that operation's success. They talked for twenty or thirty minutes. When he left the station, Júlio felt less tense. He was almost convinced he had done what had to be done. Unlike the events surrounding Amarelo's death, in Araguaia he was working for the army, in the midst of a war. It was completely different from killing someone for a handful of money and a few kilos of rice. He was trying to convince himself of this when he saw the air force helicopter roaring through the sky on its way back from the jungle. He knew the body of the woman he had killed only a few hours earlier was on board. At that moment it occurred to him that he did not even know her name. He immediately thought it would be better never to know: it would be one less name weighing on his soul.

He walked back to the boardinghouse, with a quick stop at the bakery where he bought two bottles of Coca-Cola, four bread sticks, and a half pound of cheese, in case he felt hungry later. For now, all he wanted to do was lie down and sleep, to forget the hell he had just been through.

FOR ALMOST TWENTY years, the body of the young guerrillera remained buried and forgotten in Xambioá cemetery, in Tocantins state. It was not until April 1991 that it was exhumed, when a commission made up of relatives of those killed or disappeared in the guerrilla, members of the Justice and Peace

Commission of the Archdiocese of São Paulo, and experts from the State University of Campinas (Unicamp) traveled to the town and recovered Maria Lúcia's body from the pit it had been thrown into. It had been buried without a coffin, wrapped in a parachute regiment nylon parachute. The specialists from Unicamp, led by the pathologist Fortunato Badan Palhares, director of the Department of Forensic Medicine at the time, found traces of the clothing, shoes, and accessories Maria Lúcia was wearing at the time of her death. The 0.20 bullet cartridge she had in the back pocket of her jeans was still intact.

One of those who had access to this new information was Laura Petit. Three years older than Maria Lúcia, who was the youngest in the family, Laura had given herself the mission of discovering what had happened to her sister, whom the army simply described as "disappeared" in their official version of events, as they did with all the rebels killed during the period of the guerrilla. When Laura learned that the remains of her sister had been dug up, wrapped in a nylon sheet like an animal, she could not help thinking that the same might have happened to her two brothers, Jaime and Lúcio, both of whom were also in the Araguaia guerrilla. In fact, they were both killed as well in the jungles of the region, in combat with the army. Jaime died in December 1973, aged twenty-eight, and Lúcio in April 1974, at thirty. As of today, Laura Petit has only managed to recover the mortal remains of Maria Lúcia; there is still no information as to where Jaime and Lúcio were buried.

The exhumation was only the first step in the identification of Maria Lúcia Petit da Silva's body. Back in São Paulo, Laura Petit was determined to devote all the time and effort necessary to find out if the remains the Unicamp specialists had removed from the Xambioá cemetery really were those of her sister. This was to prove a much slower and more painful process than Laura could ever have imagined. For five years, she divided her time between working as a teacher and whatever actions she thought necessary to find out if those remains were Maria Lúcia's. She lost count of the number of occasions she went to Unicamp to try to talk to the pathologist Badan Palhares and press him to speed up the resolution of the case. On one of these occasions she sat in a room in the Department of Forensic Medicine from three in the afternoon to ten o'clock at night, but had to return home without even getting to see the expert.

The months and years passed, and Maria Lúcia Petit's remains were still forgotten, bundled in plastic bags on a shelf in the cold storage at Unicamp. In the end, it was thanks to Laura's persistence that one vital piece of evidence to identify the guerrillera's remains was uncovered. At the end of April 1991, she got in touch with the dentist Jorge Tanaka, who had treated Maria Lúcia shortly before she set off for Araguaia.

Authorized by the Unicamp Department of Forensic Medicine to examine the dental arch of the remains recovered from Xambioá, Tanaka confirmed that it did indeed belong to Maria Lúcia Petit. However, the dentist's analysis had to be confirmed by Badan Palhares and his team, and this only took place five years later.

ON THE MORNING of May 15, 1996—almost twenty-four years after Maria Lúcia's death—the specialists from Unicamp called a press conference to announce their conclusions from the analyses conducted out on the remains of the guerrillera, laid out on a table covered with a blue cloth in a university lecture hall. On the left-hand side of the room, photographs of Maria Lúcia before and after she died were displayed on a wooden panel. Among the thirty or so people present were journalists, photographers, filmmakers, as well as friends and relatives of Maria Lúcia. Laura Petit was in the front row, holding hands with her mother, Dona Julieta, who was never able to accept the fact that she had lost three children in the guerrilla. Scarcely more than six feet in front of them, the pathologist Badan Palhares discussed the remains and their findings. He had a graying beard and was wearing a knee-length white coat.

In a clear, steady voice he picked up several bones from the table and explained that they were indeed part of the remains of Maria Lúcia Petit da Silva. Holding the young woman's skull in his hand, Badan Palhares used a white spatula to point out the exact spot where the fatal bullet had hit the guerrillera. Laura felt her mother squeeze her hand. Glancing at Dona Julieta, she saw she was sobbing silently. The thirty pages of the experts' findings (fourteen of them consisting entirely of photographs) concluded as follows:

WE CAN STATE THAT THERE ARE INDICATIONS THAT THE BONES ARE OF A PERSON OF THE FEMALE SEX.

THE TOP OF THE FEMUR WAS QUITE SLENDER, AS WERE THE NASAL CAVITY AND THE EYE SOCKET. THESE INDICATIONS LEAD US TO THE CONLCUSION THAT THIS IS THE SKELETON OF A WOMAN.

THE PROTUBERANCES OF THE BREASTS ARE CLEARLY VISIBLE.

As to the causes of death of Maria Lúcia Petit, the document stated that the young communist had been killed by two gunshot wounds: one to the right thigh, fired by a 7.62 rifle, and the other to the head, "in the left parietal bone, typical of the passage of a projectile from a firearm, with a trajectory from low to high and from back to front"—the shot fired by Júlio Santana.

This scientific evidence led to the very first identification of a communist killed in the Araguaia guerrilla. Even today, Maria Lúcia Petit is the only person from the rebel movement who died in combat with the armed forces to have had her body exhumed and identified, although it is estimated that close to sixty communists were killed in this guerrilla. Aged eighty-six, Dona Julieta Petit is still mourning the loss of her youngest daughter and two sons.

Following the conclusion of the case, Maria Lúcia's mortal remains were handed over to the family, who buried them in Bauru Cemetery, in São Paulo. The army never revealed the names of the men who killed the young communist on that morning of June 16, 1972. Júlio Santana never knew the name of the young woman he killed in his second homicide. Even today he considers it better that way. It is one name less to trouble his soul.

Genesis of the Hitman

EXACTLY A WEEK after he killed Maria Lúcia Petit, Júlio Santana celebrated his eighteenth birthday. On that Friday, June 23, 1972, he woke before daybreak. Ever since the day he had shot the young guerrillera, he had found it hard to sleep. Every night without exception he saw Maria's body in his nightmares. In them she had her eyes open, staring at him. He could still feel the smooth, cold skin of her ankles in the palms of his hands when he helped carry the corpse from where she had been killed to the farmer Cocoió's house. He could no longer bear to sleep and wake up in Xambioá.

He wanted to return as quickly as possible to Porto Franco. It would not be long. His uncle Cícero Santana had said he would go fetch him that morning at the boardinghouse and that soon afterward he would take him back to his parents. To get out of that hell on his birthday seemed to Júlio the best present he could ever receive.

But the hours went by, and there was no sign of Cícero. This would not be the first time his uncle had not kept his word. On several previous occasions, Carlos Marra had told him that Cícero had called, saying he would go visit his nephew in Xambioá. Each time, the wait to see his uncle had been in vain. Now, stretched out on the bed in his room, Júlio was hungry. He did not want to wait any longer for his uncle, as he knew he might not turn up. So he decided to have breakfast on his own.

He was in the bakery eating bread and cheese and drinking Coca-Cola when an army jeep pulled up outside. His uncle and Carlos Marra got out. Cícero congratulated him warmly, hugging him and slapping his back, saying he was proud of the excellent job he had done under Marra's orders in Araguaia. The police chief gave Júlio a yellow envelope. Júlio did not need to open it to know what was inside: the 100 cruzeiros he was owed for that week's work. Every Friday, Marra paid him the wage for five days' work. Júlio was convinced he would never receive so much money all at once—during the period he worked for the army, he earned 1,200 cruzeiros, a little more than five times the minimum salary at the time, which was 225 cruzeiros.

"I've got something else for you," said the chief, handing him a black plastic bag.

"What's inside?" the boy wanted to know.

"Open it and find out."

Júlio could not contain his delight when he saw it was an army uniform, with the thick long-sleeved shirt, an olive-green hat, and the boots he had been so envious of. He was keen to see how he would look dressed in the uniform and wearing the black boots.

"It's all new, see? I got it from the quartermaster and brought it straight here for you. Your uncle told me it's your birthday and I wanted to give you this present," Marra said.

"Thanks so much, chief. Really, thanks so much."

"It's nothing, Julão. You deserve it. You did a good job. If you want to stay here and carry on working with me . . ."

"No, chief. Thanks a lot, but I want to go home. I want to see my parents, my brothers and sisters, my home," said Júlio, glancing at his uncle. "I'm tired of all this trouble."

"You're right. But if you change your mind or if one day you're in Xambioá, you should look me up. Your uncle is a great friend of mine, and now you are too."

They put Júlio's things into the jeep and drove to the police station. It seemed to him that the movement of military vehicles and men in uniform was much greater than when he'd arrived in Xambioá exactly two months and twenty-five days earlier, on March 28, 1972. It is a fact that the confusion, death, and torture intensified in the region at that time. But for him that made no difference. He would soon be far from this living hell. Outside the police station, Carlos Marra got out of the jeep and said goodbye to Cícero and Júlio.

They continued in the same jeep to the town of Tocantinópolis, on the banks of the river Tocantins, the border between the states of Tocantins and Maranhão. On the other side of the river, opposite Tocantinópolis, stands Porto Franco, the region where Júlio was born. It took the army jeep almost five hours to travel the hundred miles separating Xambioá from Tocantinópolis, due to the dreadful state of the roads—all of them beaten earth—linking the two towns.

From Tocantinópolis, after almost three months, Júlio could see the muddy waters of the river Tocantins and beyond it the region where he grew up. He felt happy. Relieved. He wanted to wipe forever from his memory everything he had seen and done in Araguaia. He had even asked his uncle Cicero not to tell anyone, especially his parents, that he had taken part in the capture of the guerrillero Geraldo (as he thought José Genoino was called) and the killing of the young woman whose name he never wanted to know. To his family and friends in Porto Franco, the version he would give was that his work in the Araguaia guerrilla war had merely been to guide soldiers through the rainforest. Nothing more.

They crossed the river in a canoe that transported passengers and goods from one side to the other. They walked an hour through the forest before they came to the house of Seu Jorge and Dona Marina, Júlio's parents. From the position of the sun and the shadows of the trees on the river, he calculated it must be around five in the afternoon. Then he remembered his uncle had a watch on his left wrist, and asked him the time. It was twenty minutes to five—he had been only twenty minutes off. He was proud of himself. It was good to be back in his own universe. Without the pressure and turmoil of always having to be on the lookout for communists, he could admire the trees that grew to 130 feet in height, and the wildlife of the forest. On the way he saw a sloth, a troop of monkeys, and an enormous toucan. When they were a hundred yards from the house, he spotted his mother sitting on a log beside the river. Dona Marina was cleaning a toucanet fish to serve for supper. For the past eighty-five days, she had never had any news of Júlio. She wept night in, night out from worry over her son, who was far from her for the first time. And she prayed all the time.

The first person to see Cícero and Júlio approaching was his youngest brother Paulo, aged twelve.

"Mom, Júlio's here! Júlio's here!" the boy shouted.

Dona Marina looked back and saw her son emerging from the dense forest. She put the fish into her aluminum bowl, rinsed her hands in the river, dried them on the bermudas she was wearing, and ran toward Júlio, who was still strolling toward them. After she had kissed him lovingly and hugged him, Júlio felt protected once more. Finally he was free of the hell that was life in Xambioá. He tried to contain himself, but it was impossible. He wept and wept, his face pressed into his mother's left shoulder. He clenched his teeth in a vain attempt to stifle his sobbing. He cried so much he was left feeling weak. Seeing her son in this state, Dona Marina grew desperate: she had never seen Júlio like this before.

"What happened, Cícero? What did you and your army friends do to my boy?" she shouted at her brother-in-law. "We didn't do anything, Marina. I think it's just that Julão is happy to be back home," he replied.

"I know my son, Cícero. Something very serious must have taken place for him to be like this. But let's go in. Afterward, I want to hear all about it," said Dona Marina, leading them into the house.

Seu Jorge, Júlio's father, had gone out fishing with his other brother, the fifteen-year-old Pedro. When Dona Marina went to bring in the fish from the riverbank, Cícero took the opportunity to give his nephew some advice. He reminded Júlio that he himself had asked him not to mention anything of what had happened in the jungles of Araguaia. If that was really what he wanted, he had to control himself and stop crying. He would have to tell his parents he had wept because of his emotion at returning home after so long away, and that he had not had any problems during the time he had been serving in the army. The uniform and the boots were proof that he had been well treated by the military. Júlio liked what his uncle told him, and that was exactly what he told his parents over supper that night. Before they ate, Dona Marina said how happy she was to have her son back on the very day of his eighteenth birthday. They all sang "Happy Birthday" and kissed and hugged him. After the meal, Seu Jorge, Dona Marina, Pedro, and Paulo wanted to hear tales of Júlio's experiences in Araguaia. He said he was too tired and wanted to go to sleep.

"Tomorrow I'll tell you whatever you like," he said, before falling into his hammock.

He slept well and peacefully, in a way he had not done for almost three months. Even the air seemed different, purer. Stretched out in the gently swaying hammock, he could hear the cries of the wildlife in the jungle. If he looked around, he could see his brothers in their hammocks, lit by the lamp hanging from the roof of the straw hut. He felt an immense peace. It was really good to know that the next day he would not have to hunt communists or spend hours with an ax beneath a sweltering sun working for the military. He would not be forced to see dead bodies displayed in public spaces or prisoners tortured to death. And most important of all: he would not have to kill anyone. Júlio was happy. That night, the last thought that went through his mind was that the very first thing he would do when he woke up the next morning was to jump into his canoe to go and see Ritinha.

AFTER BREAKFAST the following morning he got into his canoe and paddled to Ritinha's village. It was a scorching hot Saturday with clear skies and few clouds. As he paddled along, he remembered the day he made the same journey to lose his virginity with his sweetheart. He was pleased to see that nothing had changed in Porto Franco. The forest, the river and the local villages all looked the same. He thought Ritinha would not have changed either. She must still be beautiful and would be dying to see him again. As he paddled, he thought of her dark skin, her big black eyes, fleshy mouth, and sturdy thighs.

When he reached the village, he beached the canoe and sat on the bank, studying the houses. There was no sign of Ritinha. He was so anxious he decided to go and knock on her door. As he was walking toward his sweetheart's house, he saw her come running out, holding hands with Odila, her best friend. They were both wearing only shorts and a T-shirt. They ran down to the river and jumped into the water to ease the heat of that stifling morning.

While the two girls were playing in the water, Júlio got back into his canoe and slowly approached them. He paddled head down, hiding his face beneath the brim of the army hat Carlos Marra had given him the day before. When he was about ten yards from them, he took off the hat and raised his head.

"Hey, pretty girl," he said.

Júlio saw a strange expression in his sweetheart's eyes. He was sure she had recognized him at once, but even so Ritinha seemed frightened, almost uncomfortable at seeing him at such a short distance from her. Her reaction was completely different from what he had imagined. In his dreams, their reencounter began with lots of kisses and hugs. But she was staring at him as though he were a stranger. Júlio went closer still, and saw Ritinha clutch Odila's hand as if she needed her friend's help to confront him. He could not understand what was going on.

"What's wrong, Ritinha? It looks as if you're not pleased to see me," said Júlio.

"It's nothing," she said, with a wan smile and without letting go of her friend's hand.

"I thought you'd be happy to see me after all this time."

"The thing is . . ."

"The thing is what?"

"You disappeared without saying a word, Júlio. I thought you had got what you wanted from me and had abandoned me."

"You were wrong, Ritinha. I was traveling. I went to do a job, but I couldn't tell you about it. But now I'm here."

Odila interrupted their conversation with words that left the boy stunned.

"It's too late now, Júlio. She already has another love."

Ritinha's head was bowed; she was staring at the muddy river flowing by. Júlio was silent too: he had no idea what to say. Or to think. If Ritinha really did have another love, all the time he had spent thinking of her during the months in Araguaia had been useless. If he had known, he would have taken more advantage of the girls in "Vietnam." He wouldn't have felt so guilty about having spent those few minutes in bed with Cibele. Ritinha was still looking down without saying a word. This irritated him still more.

"Is it true? You've found another love?" he asked.

Ritinha's reply was a slight nod of the head. Júlio felt a wave of bitter rage sweep over him, constricting his heart. He felt like jumping out of the canoe, taking hold of her by the arms, and shaking her as hard as he could. But he controlled himself.

"I want to hear you say it, Ritinha. Have you already found another love?"

"I have," came the scarcely audible reply.

"And who is this guy?"

"You don't know him. He's not from here."

"You're worthless, like my uncle said. You only want people to do dirty things with you."

Ritinha was still looking down, holding hands with her friend. Breathing heavily, Júlio picked up the paddle and drove it into the water, ready to start back home. When he was thirty yards from his sweetheart, he turned to look back and shouted as loudly as he could:

"Ritinha, you whore!"

This was the last time he ever saw the girl. From that day on, he avoided going past the village where she lived. Whenever he was forced to do so he stared at the jungle on the far side of the river as he paddled by. He went home, his heart aching with rage. He was sorry he had not shaken Ritinha by the shoulders as he'd been tempted to do. And above all, sorry for all the time he had wasted thinking of her and imagining she was doing the same. For a moment he thought that if he had been carrying a weapon he would have been capable of shooting Ritinha. That was what she deserved, but he would never do that. He had already decided he would never kill anyone ever again.

Júlio spent the rest of the day in silence. His parents and brothers were interested in the work he had done in Araguaia, but he said he was still tired from the journey and that uncle Cícero could tell them everything.

After lunch, he left to go for a walk in the forest. Cícero said he would go with him so that they could hunt an animal for supper, but Júlio preferred to go on his own. And without his rifle. He could not stop thinking about Ritinha. A dark hatred oppressed him. He found some Brazil nuts in the undergrowth and sat on the ground to eat them. He tried to distract his attention peering up into the trees to spot the creatures of the forest, but could not get the idea of doing Ritinha some harm out of his head. She could not get away with what she had done. At the same time, he realized that his anger toward his former sweetheart meant he had stopped thinking about the dark times he'd known in Xambioá and the Araguaia jungle. He even felt encouraged that maybe it would not be impossible to forget that hell entirely. His soul felt lighter. Compared to everything he had lived through in Araguaia, Ritinha's betrayal ought not to affect him so much.

He returned home as the sun was setting. The sky was streaked with purple, red, and orange. Pedro and Paulo were bathing in the river. Dona Marina, Seu Jorge, and Cícero were sitting on a log outside the house, deep in conversation. Júlio pulled off his shirt and threw it into his mother's lap, then ran off toward his brothers. Before plunging into the river, he gave a childish whoop of delight and laughed in a way he had not done for a long while. He remained in the water playing with Pedro and Paulo until Dona Marina called them in for supper. The boys dried themselves off and put on their clothes on the wooden platform at the front of the house. When he went inside, Júlio saw a chocolate cake—his favorite—with a white candle, in the center of the room. The whole family began to sing "Happy Birthday to You."

"But my birthday was yesterday," he said, feeling immensely happy.

"But you arrived by surprise yesterday, and I didn't have time to make anything, my son," said Dona Marina. She then cut the cake and offered the first slice to the birthday boy.

"Do you have any Coca-Cola, Mom?" asked Júlio, munching on the cake.

"My boy, you know we don't have the money for such luxuries. I've got some of that grape Ki-Suco you like so much," she said, serving him a glassful.

In Xambioá at least I could drink Coca-Cola at any time of day, thought Júlio, but he said nothing so as not to upset his parents. In the lamplight they all ate cake, a piece of fried fish, and talked. For the first time, Júlio told his family some of the stories from his time in Araguaia. He mentioned Tonho's strange lisp, the army trucks and jeeps, and told them all the details he could recall of the emotional ride he had in a helicopter. He told them how difficult he found it to sleep in the boardinghouse bed, and of the big aluminum box Uncle Cícero had in his house, which froze water.

"And he even had a glass ball hanging from the ceiling that lights the whole house. It's much better than this lamp," he said. His parents and brothers listened to him keenly. Júlio felt he was the most important person in the world. He picked up the bag he'd brought from Xambioá, ran out of the house, and put on the military uniform Carlos Marra had given him. He added the army hat and boots and came back in. When she saw her son, Dona Marina gave a huge smile and said she had never seen such a fine-looking boy. Seu Jorge praised him as well, saying Júlio looked just like an army general. Pedro and Paulo came over to touch their brother's uniform.

"Cícero, why don't you take Júlio to be a military policeman in Imperatriz, like you?" Dona Marina suggested to her brother-in-law.

"I think that's a great idea, but it's up to him," replied Cícero.

"Do it, son. We're going to miss you, but there's no future for you here. You'll die without ever leaving this backwater," Seu Jorge said.

"But don't go right away, will you? First you need to spend some time here with us. You've been away a long while," Dona Marina insisted.

Júlio heard all this without saying a word. It made him think. He believed it might be a good thing to go to Imperatriz and join the military police. But he was very afraid of going through something similar to his experiences in Araguaia. He did not trust his uncle Cícero the way he once had.

After talking a long while, they all settled down to sleep. Before getting into his hammock, Júlio put the shirt, the boots, and the hat back in the plastic bag, but kept the trousers on. As he lay down, he could feel something in the right-hand back pocket. It was the envelope with all the money he'd brought from Xambioá. He remembered that he had no idea how much he had accumulated during almost three months' work there. By the lamp's dim light, he counted all the notes and coins: it came to 920 cruzeiros and 80 cents, after all his expenses in the town. So much money! He had never imagined he would have such riches. He was sure that not even his father had held such a quantity in his hands all at once. He thought that in the end, all the suffering he had gone through in Araguaia had been worth it. The sleepless nights, the fear, and even the deaths he had witnessed—even that of Maria Lúcia Petit—had not been in vain.

A week later, he set out for Imperatriz with Cícero. They traveled in the truck of one of his uncle's friends. Júlio said almost nothing throughout the journey, while Cícero and the driver chatted about soccer, women, and the situation with the

Araguaia guerrilla. The military were still catching and killing communists and any local inhabitants who collaborated with them.

One of the most terrifying events of recent days, said the driver, had been the beheading of a young guerrillero. The soldiers had strolled around the streets of Xambioá carrying the man's head. This story disturbed Júlio less than it would have before his stay in Araguaia. He thought the whole thing was terrible, but had seen even worse things with his own eyes.

When they reached Cícero's house, Júlio heard his uncle say that it wouldn't be as easy to join the military police as Seu Jorge and Dona Marina imagined. Júlio would have to pass an examination set by the force, and the date for the next round of exams had not even been decided yet.

"So what am I going to do here, Uncle?" the boy asked.

"You're going to work. Isn't that what you came here to do?"

"Work as what? I don't know how to do anything."

"Yes you do. You know how to shoot very well. Your aim is—"

"No, Uncle. You can forget that. I don't want to know any more about that business of killing people. I've already told you that," said Júlio, getting up from the sofa to fetch a glass of water from the fridge.

It took Cícero three days to convince his nephew to accompany him on a contract. He was going to kill a man because of an argument on a soccer field. The person who was contracting him had been punched in the face during a game in front of everyone. On the field, Leandor, who had received the blow, had threatened his attacker: "I'll kill you!" Since he didn't have the courage to do it himself, the youngster, the son of a big landowner in the region, had paid Cícero to do it.

"You're going to kill the guy just because he hit someone in the face?" Júlio asked nervously.

"No, Julão. I'm going to kill the guy because someone paid me to do it. You have to learn something. In this business, it doesn't matter if the target is a great guy or a pest. I don't want to know if he punched somebody in the face or raped someone's daughter. What matters is that I'm being paid to do the job."

Júlio was scared at how coldly his uncle could say this, but remembered that he admired his strength and courage. Not everyone can kill a man without being afraid or feeling remorse or sadness. You had to be strong to do that.

On the day of the murder Júlio and his uncle left the house before sunrise. They were both wearing hats: "to hide your face," Cícero explained. He took Júlio on his bike to the neighborhood where the victim lived, about three miles away. They came to a halt about a hundred yards from the house where Aníbal lived. He was about six foot three, short and stout, dark-complexioned and with graying hair. They waited almost two hours sitting on the forecourt of a gas station until Aníbal came out. Leaving the bike chained to a lamppost, they began to follow him, keeping him at least fifty yards in front of them. After about a mile they came to the grocery store where the man worked. After another three hours' waiting, Júlio felt hungry and suggested they buy some crackers and a cold drink in the store. Cícero wouldn't hear of it, arguing that they should never be seen by Aníbal before the zero hour. "That could ruin the entire plan," he said. At lunchtime, Aníbal crossed the road for something to eat at a bar opposite. Less than an hour later, he was back behind the counter in the grocer's. Júlio was suffering: he couldn't bear all this waiting. How long would they have to stay there, sitting in the middle of the road, without doing anything?

"Julão, in this kind of profession, patience is as important as good marksmanship. If you get nervous, you can ruin the whole thing. You need to learn."

Júlio felt confused. While he was upset by the way his uncle was constantly talking down to him, he was somehow proud to be living this experience. And what most disturbed him: he was beginning to feel a certain admiration and respect for the work his hitman uncle carried out. He didn't know how this could be possible, but that was what he felt. The noise of the cars on the beaten earth streets and the busy comings and goings of pedestrians no longer bothered him. In Xambioá he'd gotten used to this dreadful chaos. He was anxious to see how his uncle would put an end to this guy's life.

At exactly six o'clock, he heard the ringing of the bells in the church two blocks behind the grocery store. Ten or fifteen minutes later, Aníbal and another man closed the store, pulling down big red shutters. The two men crossed the street to the bar. Júlio and Cícero went over to the entrance, but stayed outside. Cícero glanced quickly inside.

"They're sitting at the counter drinking a beer. They won't be long," he said.

"How do you know?" asked Júlio.

"Because there are two empty tables. If they were going to stay long, they would have sat at a table and not at the counter."

Cícero was right. Fifteen minutes later, the two men emerged from the bar. They said goodbye and went their separate ways. Cícero had already sent his nephew on ahead, toward Aníbal's house.

"Why's that, Uncle?"

"When he gets near you, strike up a conversation with him," Cícero told him.

"What do you mean? What am I going to say?"

"I don't know, Julão. Say anything. Ask him something that makes him stop to talk to you."

"But Uncle—"

"Invent some story or other. You're intelligent. You'll think of something."

It was already growing dark in Imperatriz. Without looking up from the road, Júlio racked his brains to think of what he could say to make Aníbal stop without scaring him. The minutes went by and nothing occurred to him. He saw Aníbal turn the corner, and could sense his heart pounding. His body was covered in a cold sweat. Aníbal was walking toward him, and he still had no idea what to say. Shortly after, Cícero also turned the corner, about fifty yards behind the victim. With every step the man took, Júlio's nervousness increased. By now he was only fifteen or twenty yards away. Júlio went up to him and asked:

"Do you know where I can buy a Coca-Cola?" he said, not looking at him.

"What's that, boy? Speak more slowly," said Aníbal.

"I want to buy a Coca-Cola. Do you know where I can get one?"

"Oh yes. There's a bar close to here. You just have to turn right—"

Their conversation was interrupted by a sharp explosion. Júlio, who was still staring down at the ground, saw Aníbal's body fall at his feet. Terrified, he took a step back. The back of the head of the man his uncle had just shot was covered in blood. Júlio felt his sight grow dim. Cícero took him by the left arm and the two of them ran off down the road. After two blocks, they turned to the left and came to a halt. Júlio still could not speak. His uncle took off the checked shirt he was wearing, leaving only his white undershirt. He told Júlio to take off his shirt and hat. They got on the bike and returned home, with Cícero pedaling steadily as though nothing had happened. Júlio couldn't forget the image of their victim sprawled at his feet, his head bathed in red. His uncle, though, displayed an amazing calm. How could he be so serene after taking somebody's life? It was so cold: or was it courage? Straddling the bike, holding onto the saddle with both hands, Júlio saw people walking along the dusty roads. He was sure those ordinary people did not know what it meant to kill someone. There was no room for such a risky, exciting act. He felt an involuntary pride at having taken part in this intrepid action. After following Aníbal all day, he and his uncle had succeeded in doing their job. And most importantly, they had avoided attracting anyone's attention. These were the thoughts going around in Júlio's mind when he heard Cícero ask what he had said to make their victim come to a stop in the street.

"I asked if he knew where I could buy a Coca-Cola."

"Very good, Julão. You're much more expert than I thought."

"Do you really think so?"

"Of course, kid. That story about Coke was great. You were born for this kind of work. You've got a talent for it."

Júlio did not like to hear his uncle Cícero say he was born to be a killer. And yet at the same time he was proud at the thought that he had some kind of special talent. That night he stayed at his uncle's. They ate rice and a fried egg and talked until one in the morning. By the time Júlio went to bed his uncle had persuaded him to become a professional hitman. Júlio found his uncle's arguments convincing. If he worked as a gunman, he could travel, get to know different places, live exciting experiences, and at the same time earn a good living. His uncle told him that for example by killing Aníbal he had earned five hundred cruzeiros. In a single day, his uncle had gained more than half of all that he himself had gained from almost three months' work in Araguaia. The business of killing people could be difficult, but the money compensated for that. Even the fear the boy expressed at being arrested was dismissed by Cícero. Out here in the interior, he said, the police did not get involved with gunmen. Before he fell asleep in his hammock, Júlio was convinced he would be able to join the world of hired killers. However, by the time he woke up the next morning he had changed his mind.

When he got out of his hammock, he saw his uncle in the kitchen. From the sounds and smells he guessed his uncle was frying eggs. Júlio went to the bathroom and as he urinated he thought he did not want to lead the life of a killer. The possibility of becoming rich as his uncle said was tempting. The adventures he might have in that kind of work also seemed very interesting to him. But he did not want to always have to bear the weight of killing someone simply for money. He washed his face in the aluminum basin, put his hands under the faucet and wet his hair. He ate two fried egg sandwiches and drank a cup of coffee. He was silent the whole time. Cícero wanted to know what was bothering him.

"You went to bed so happy, Julão, so enthusiastic about our work."

"I'm not sure, Uncle. I don't think I want to take up that kind of thing."

"Julão, don't keep thinking about it. Last night we talked it over and everything seemed settled."

"I know. But I don't want to spend my life killing people, Uncle. I've already killed two persons, and my stomach still churns when I remember it."

"That's normal, kid. Over time you'll get used to the work and won't feel that sort of thing anymore. Trust me."

"I'm not sure, Uncle. I'm not sure."

Cícero got up out of his aluminum chair, went into the living room, and called his nephew, who was still in the kitchen. They sat down on the red and black sofa and began a conversation that Júlio would never forget. He listened as his uncle said there was nothing immoral about the work he did. Yes, what he did was a sin. But as the priest had already told him, God forgave everything. In the case of a killing, it was enough to say ten Hail Marys and twenty Our Fathers and his soul would be cleansed. And besides, if they did not fulfill any particular contract, the victim would die anyway.

"What do you mean, Uncle?"

"If we turn the contract down, they will hire someone else to kill the guy, Julão. There's no shortage of people happy to shoot some poor jerk to earn five hundred cruzeiros or more."

"I'm not sure, Uncle."

"Julão, just think about it. I earned everything I have from what I've made as a hitman. You're always saying you want to have a house like mine, with a radio, fridge, electric light, good food. If you start working with me, you'll have all that before too long."

"But you still have your job in the military police, don't you?"

"I do. But what I earn from that is next to nothing. For example, I got the money to buy my motorboat from the jobs

I do outside the force. Imagine yourself with your own boat: you'll be able to travel up and down all the rivers whenever you like."

Júlio listened to all this without taking his eyes off the poster of Our Lady of Aparecida that Cícero had hanging from a nail on the wall of his living room. He thought that the saint would not like him to join his uncle as a contract killer. On the other hand, if God pardoned that kind of sin, it couldn't be all that serious. According to Cícero, it was quite simple. All you had to do was to accept the contract, take the money, kill the guy, and pray ten Hail Marys and twenty Our Fathers. Making sure they were said in that order.

He decided to accept his uncle's offer. If at any moment and for any reason he changed his mind, all he had to do was to go back to his parents' house in Porto Franco, return to the peaceful life he'd led on the banks of the river Tocantins.

That night he spent hours listening to his uncle explain all he knew about the work of a professional killer. They sat on the wooden floorboards leaning back against the sofa. The transistor radio was on all the time, but the boy was so caught up in what his uncle was saying that he didn't even hear the music. He can only remember having heard for the first time a song that would remain with him all his life, the refrain of which was: "I'm going to get you out of here. I'm going to take you to stay with me." He wanted to know who was singing; Cícero said it was Brazil's best singer: Odair José. But he immediately went back to the topic that really interested him. Before anything else, Júlio needed to learn a list that his uncle called the Code of Honor of the hitman.

"These are things you should never do, whatever happens. Even if you are offered lots of money," said Cícero.

The list that Júlio managed to learn in less than an hour contained five prohibitions:

DO NOT KILL A PREGNANT WOMAN.

"Unless you did not know she was pregnant," Cícero stressed.

DO NOT STEAL ANYTHING FROM THE VICTIM.

"We're gunmen, not thieves."

DO NOT KILL OTHER GUNMEN.

"We have to respect our professional colleagues."

DO NOT TAKE ANY JOB ON CREDIT.

"Death does not wait."

DO NOT KILL A PERSON WHO IS ASLEEP.

"That would be cowardice."

WHEN JÚLIO TOLD his uncle he had memorized this unusual code of honor, Cícero went on to give him tips which in his view would be extremely important for his nephew to succeed in this line of work. The first was for the boy to save as much as he could in order to buy a motorbike as soon as possible. Cícero said this was the perfect vehicle for a hitman. It was agile, rapid, and economical. In addition, the helmet would help keep his face hidden from any possible witnesses. He himself was about to buy one; he hadn't done so yet because he'd used his savings to buy the boat and the outboard motor. Another recommendation was that Júlio should always use the same weapon. That would give him more security and precision in his shooting. Raising his shirt, Cícero pulled a .38 revolver from his waistband.

"It's yours. From now on, this is the weapon you will use," he said, handing it to him.

"But Uncle, I've never fired a revolver. I only know how to use a rifle," said the boy.

"That's why I'm giving it to you now. Early every morning I want you to take the revolver and go and practice your marksmanship in the forest. I'll only give you your first job when you're good at it."

"Okay."

"But remember one thing."

"What's that?"

"I only want you to learn to shoot well with the revolver so that you'll feel more sure of yourself. In our work, only rarely will you need to shoot someone from a distance. The ideal is for you to kill the person from close up, as I did with Aníbal."

"Why?"

"Because it's very important that your shot be accurate. And preferably to the head. From farther away there's a risk that you might miss the target or for someone or something to get into your line of sight. But you'll learn all this over time. I'm sure you'll become an excellent marksman. We're going to earn a lot of money together."

Cícero had some more tips to offer his nephew:

DO NOT TALK MUCH WITH THE VICTIM.

DO NOT TALK WITH PEOPLE LIVING IN THE VICINITY OF THE VICTIM.

AVOID GETTING INTO ANY KIND OF TROUBLE, EITHER WHERE YOU DO THE JOB OR IN THE PLACE WHERE YOU LIVE.

"It's very important to be known where you live as a quiet person. That will avoid suspicion," his uncle taught him.

NEVER USE YOUR REAL NAME WHEN DOING YOUR JOB.

"It's preferable to use the name of an acquaintance. It's easier to memorize and to respond when someone calls you by the false name."

Júlio did his best to learn all the rules and tips his uncle had suggested. He also made a great effort to quickly learn to use the revolver. In two weeks, he felt he was ready. In the third, he undertook his first job as a professional hitman. Cícero put his nephew on a bus and sent him to the town of Açailândia, in the state of Maranhão, some forty miles from Imperatriz. He was to kill a man called Caetano, who owed 2,000 cruzeiros to a local businessman, whose name Júlio never knew—and never wanted to know. He spent the whole journey securing the revolver in his waistband. In order to hide his weapon he was wearing a loose undershirt with a shirt on top. He also wore a straw hat to hide his face. In Açailândia a skinny young boy who looked a bit younger than him was waiting at the bus stop. The boy hardly spoke, but took him to a street market where Caetano was selling fruit and vegetables behind a wooden counter.

"He's the one," said the boy, pointing to the street vendor, then left him.

Júlio was all on his own. Taking cover behind a cart filled with watermelons, he studied the man he was to kill. Caetano looked like a good guy. About five foot six, he had big eyes in a sharply defined face, and sparse dark hair. He served anyone who came to his stall with a broad smile. Even before he used his revolver, Júlio felt sorry for him. He recalled his uncle's words: *In this business, it doesn't matter if the fellow hit someone in the face or raped someone's daughter. What matters is that I've been paid to do the job.* Júlio wished he could be just as cool about it. Just as courageous. Besides, Cícero had told him he'd already received the money for killing Caetano. There was no going back. Júlio was so nervous he considered the possibility of shooting him right there, in the middle of the market. He would shoot the vendor in the head, run off, and jump on the first bus back to Imperatriz. But he soon concluded that would be too risky.

He decided to do the same as his uncle had done when he shot Aníbal. He waited for Caetano to close up shop and collect what was left of the fruit and vegetables. Then he followed him through the dusty streets of Açailândia, keeping a distance of about thirty yards between them. Caetano was walking along with a friend, and Júlio needed to wait until his victim was on his own. He almost despaired when he saw Caetano say goodbye to his companion and go into an unpainted wooden hut that had no brick walls and only a black plastic sheet for a roof. Júlio did not know what to do. How could he kill someone in their own home? Better to give up, return to Imperatriz, and leave killing him until another day. But if he did that he would have to go through all this torment a second time. And he would have to admit failure in his first job as a hitman. He decided he would only leave Açailândia once he had killed Caetano.

It was growing dark, and his target was still inside his house. Júlio sat waiting on the far side of the street, beneath a guava tree. There was no electricity in the town: the street was pitch black. The only points of light came from lamps inside some of the shacks, spilling out into the darkness. Time was passing, and nothing was happening. Júlio had what he thought was a brilliant idea, but would need a lot of courage and a cool head to put into practice. He would go up to Caetano's house and call out to him. When the street vendor came to the door, he would shoot him in the head. Then he would run into the thick undergrowth that lay behind the line of houses. Still seated under the guava, Júlio looked up and down the street. No one about. He walked over to Caetano's shack. His heart was racing. His hands were bathed in cold sweat.

"Seu Caetano!" he shouted, deepening his voice to disguise it.

"Who is it?" the street vendor shouted back.

"I have a message for you, it's urgent."

"I'm coming."

Standing outside the door, Júlio pulled the revolver from his belt. As his uncle had instructed him, he snapped open the chamber to make sure it was loaded. Hiding his hands behind his back, he waited for Caetano to open the door. He would shoot only once, at his head. He heard the window next to the door being raised.

"What is it?" asked Caetano.

Júlio wanted to get this over with as quickly as possible, and thought of firing without a word. But that was impossible. His body did not seem to obey his brain. He was paralyzed with nerves. He could not even talk properly: the words came tumbling out.

"I want to open a stall in the market. Do you know what I need to do?" he managed to say.

"What are you talking about? You said you had a message for me."

"I only wanted to know if you could help me," stammered Júlio, going over to the window.

"I'm just a vendor. If you want to open a stall, you'll have to speak to the people who organize the market."

Júlio pulled his right hand from behind his back and pointed the revolver at Caetano's head. The man's eyes opened wide and he turned pale. He took a deep breath and his lips began to move, as if he wanted to say something. He did not have time to do so. Júlio pulled the trigger and saw the bullet enter just above Caetano's left eye. He did not wait to see the lifeless body fall to the ground, but ran into the undergrowth. As he ran, he recited the ten Hail Marys and twenty Our Fathers that were meant to relieve his soul of the weight of the death of that poor guy. Yet the more Júlio prayed, the guiltier he became. He repeated the prayers a second time. He was bathed in sweat. He was very hungry and thirsty: he had not eaten anything since breakfast that morning. He dropped to the ground covered in dry leaves and went on praying until he fell asleep. It was June 27, 1972, and Júlio Santana had just carried out his first job as a professional hitman.

The next morning, he caught the bus back to Imperatriz. He felt strangely proud at having done his job so professionally. Not everyone had the courage to put a bullet into someone's head at only a yard's distance. When he returned to his uncle's house, he told him everything he could remember. Cícero praised him for his idea of calling his victim to the front door. He also approved of the patience Júlio had shown by waiting for hours under the guava tree until the right moment arrived. And he assured his nephew that he need not worry, because God had definitely forgiven him. Smiling proudly, he took a wad of banknotes from his shirt pocket and gave it to Júlio. The youngster counted out 300 cruzeiros.

"I thought it was going to be more, Uncle," he said.

"You don't think that's much, Julão? If you do two contracts like that a month, you'll earn six hundred cruzeiros. That's more than half of what you got for three months' work in Araguaia."

"I know, Uncle. But you got five hundred for killing that guy Aníbal close to here."

"So what?"

"I thought that, since the job I did was in another town, there would be more money in it."

"That's how things are, Julão. Every contract has a different price. But I'm glad to see you're concerned about the money. That's good," said Cícero with a smile.

That night, Júlio counted the money several times before falling asleep. To earn 300 cruzeiros for a day's work was something he'd never imagined to be possible. Besides that, he had enjoyed the emotion he experienced when he killed Caetano. The fear, the tension, the nervousness, his racing heart had somehow made him feel good. He wanted to have more adventures like that. He wanted to earn more money.

487 Recorded Deaths

THIS WAS NOT the first time the thought had crossed Júlio Santana's mind. How many people had he killed in his life? He woke up that Sunday, April 16, 2006, determined to calculate the figure. It would not be hard. He only needed to find the notebook where he wrote down every job he had done, which he kept in an old knapsack hidden behind a wardrobe. Since he only began to keep a tally in 1974—three years after his first killing—three of his victims would not be on the list. The fisherman Amarelo, the guerrillera Maria Lúcia Petit, and the street vendor Caetano would be missing from his book.

As usual on Sundays, Júlio spent the whole day at home in Porto Franco in Maranhão state. He had returned to live there in 1984, the year he was married. He lived with his wife and two children, a boy of eighteen and a girl aged twelve. Their eldest boy, who would have been twenty-one in March 2006, died in a motorbike accident in October 2004 in Imperatriz. Even now, Júlio believes that the death of his firstborn was a punishment from God for all the wrongs he had committed in his life.

He did not want his family to see him carrying out this strange calculation. He waited until his wife and daughter had left the house to attend the morning service in the Assembly of God church, and for his son to go and play soccer. When Júlio was alone, he went to his bedroom and dragged the wardrobe across the cement floor. The knapsack was covered in dust. He turned his head to one side, held his breath, and beat the bag with his hands. Before he opened it, he wanted to make sure that nobody would come into the house and catch him unawares. He went to the front door and looked down the street. All he saw were four or five kids playing soccer on the beaten earth road. Closing the two windows and doors at the front and back of the house, he pulled out the notebook. On the cover was a picture of Donald Duck. The yellowing pages inside contained the names of everyone he had killed since March 1974, together with the date and place where he had carried out the contract, how much he had received, and the names of both client and victim.

He sat on the three-seater brown sofa and opened the rolled-up notebook. Before beginning the count, he looked around the whole room. On his left was another sofa, for two people. Opposite him in the middle of the room stood a glass-topped table, with beyond it a cherrywood cabinet with a twenty-inch TV screen, the stereo and DVD system, on which he had just paid the last installment and had offered to his children as a Christmas present. In one corner stood the dining table, also made of cherry wood, with four chairs. He had never understood why his wife insisted on keeping a glass vase with two plastic roses in the middle of the table. On one wall was a poster of the Zezé Di Camargo and Luciano duo that his son was a fan of, and another of the Flamengo soccer team that had been World Club champions in 1981. Still clutching the notebook, Júlio stood up and went into the kitchen. He looked at the blue stove with four burners, the white refrigerator, and the microwave next to the wall that had stopped working almost a year earlier. A clay filter shared the aluminum sink with a pile of plates and pans. He took a quick look into the children's bedroom (they were constantly saying that they wanted separate rooms) and the one he shared with his wife. She'd been complaining for two years that the children's furniture was too old.

Júlio returned to the living room and sat down again on the big sofa. The notebook was still rolled up in his right hand. Before starting to read the list of people he had killed, he recalled how he had entered the world of hired killers seduced above all by his uncle Cícero's promises that this line of work would make him a rich man. From everything he had just looked over in his house, he had not come anywhere near that. Yet he believed he lived far better than his parents and the majority of his friends, who had never had enough money to buy things like a big TV, a DVD player, or a sound system. In addition, he had his own canoe with an outboard motor, and a car, a 1985 blue Fiat 147, which he had received as payment for a service he had carried out. And he had also managed to save almost 100,000 reis he was planning to use to buy a plot of land and build a new house a long way from Maranhão. Somewhere he could live in peace with his wife and children. But at the age of fifty-one, of which close to thirty-five had been spent exclusively as a hired killer, he thought that this was very little compared to all the trouble and misery he'd seen and done in his life. If he had known he would end up like this, he would never have heeded his uncle's advice.

He stretched out his legs until he was resting the heels of his feet on the table, and lay back on the sofa. He began leafing through the notebook, page after page. He never thought it would be so difficult to discover how many people he had killed. As he read through the names of his victims, his mind took him back to the day and the place of the crime. Even today he still cannot figure how he also managed to recall the tiniest details, such as the clothes his victim was wearing at the time of his death, whether it was hot or cold, what he had eaten before carrying out his mission.

Occasionally the circumstances of the crime and where it took place made the experience unforgettable. This was what Júlio felt when he read the name "João Baiano" (literally João from Bahia) in the notebook. Written in brackets in shaky capital letters was a description of his victim: black, well-built, five foot six, with a gold tooth on the top left of his mouth. João Baiano was the first of four men Júlio killed in the famous gold mines of Serra Pelada in the south of Pará state.

From mid-1980, his uncle Cícero had been telling him about the huge numbers of people who were flocking from all over Brazil to the Serra Pelada in the hope of finding gold and getting rich. At the time, the recent discovery of gold deposits had turned the region into a sort of El Dorado, where some twenty thousand men excavated the Serra dos Carajás by hand in search of nuggets of gold.

The influx was so great that little more than a year later—September 1981—there were almost eighty thousand gold prospectors living and working in Serra Pelada—more than lived in most towns in the rest of Pará state. According to Cícero, the rewards and the ambitions of all these miners were creating disputes that could only be resolved by bullets.

"It's a fantastic opportunity for us to make money, Julão," his uncle told him as they talked one day in Imperatriz in the month of March 1981.

"Do you think so?" replied Júlio, who by now was twenty-six years old but was still living with his uncle, who continued to treat him as if he were a teenager.

"Of course, kid. And we could even be paid in gold. Think of that! Coming home with your pockets full of gold."

"Is it really that easy?"

"Do you remember when I left here last week saying I had a job to do?"

"Yes, I do."

"Well, I went to Serra Pelada to kill a guy who had stolen gold from someone else. That happens all the time there."

"And how much were you paid?"

Cícero got up from the sofa, went into his bedroom and came back with his left fist closed.

"This is what I was paid," said his uncle, opening his hand and revealing a gold nugget scarcely bigger than a grain of corn.

"Uncle, I can't believe you killed a guy for so little," said Júlio, unable to keep himself from laughing.

"Don't be silly, Julão. There's eleven grams of gold here. Do you know how much that's worth?"

"No. I know gold is worth a lot, but that tiny piece of rock . . ." replied Júlio, still smiling broadly.

"Of course you don't. This nugget here is worth 9,900 cruzeiros, Julão. Nine thousand nine hundred cruzeiros," Cícero repeated in a firm voice, almost thrusting the gold into his nephew's face. Júlio was impressed that this tiny nugget could be worth so much—at the time, the minimum wage in Brazil was 8,460 cruzeiros and one gram of gold was sold in Serra Pelada for 900 cruzeiros. Two months earlier, he had received 6,000 cruzeiros for killing a farmer in Esperantina in Tocantins state, contracted by a big landowner who was angry at his land being invaded by a group of peasant farmers. To kill another poor guy and get paid in gold seemed like a good idea to Júlio. He came to believe that having one of those nuggets, however small, would be an important step toward realizing his dream of becoming a rich man.

He followed Cícero's advice and agreed to travel to Serra Pelada. In the end, however, their trip to the largest non-industrial gold mine in the world only took place a year later, in February 1982, when his uncle told him he'd been contracted to carry out three jobs there. Cícero would do two of them and Júlio, as he did not have as much experience, could take care of the third. He would receive 5,000 cruzeiros.

They left Imperatriz for Marabá, in the southeast of Pará state. It was a hundred miles of potholed roads, almost half of them only beaten earth. The dry weather meant that the traffic of trucks and omnibuses crammed with people heading for Pará's El Dorado raised a constant fine red dust. This irritated Júlio's eyes and gave him a constant cough. During the four hours the journey lasted, he smoked almost half a pack of Continental cigarettes. He had picked up the smoking habit from his uncle Cícero. He remembered hating the bitter taste of the first cigarette he put in his mouth when he was nineteen. But Cícero always told him that smoking made a man stronger and more courageous, so he decided to force himself to enjoy it. He still said that he didn't like cigarettes, but that cigarettes seemed to like him a lot.

When they reached Marabá, Júlio found a town that was far busier than when he had been there for the first time three years earlier to kill two farmers involved in disputes with big land-owners. (Even today, Pará is the state with the greatest number of murders related to land conflicts.) Marabá was crammed with cars, trucks, and buses. People walked around the streets with bags, knapsacks, and saddlebags in their arms or on their backs. The hubbub was constant. A woman was a rare sight in the midst of this crowd. Almost all of them were men, from different parts of Brazil, ready to do anything to "strike it lucky," as the gold prospectors described those who succeeded in getting rich from the gold.

This huge mass of people had emptied the shelves of the markets and bakeries. Cícero and Júlio wanted to buy supplies before they set off for Serra Pelada, but could not find any beans, pasta, sugar, biscuits, or oil. All they managed to purchase were five kilos of rice, two of dried meat, salt, flour, two tins of guava juice, and a pack of cigarettes. Before boarding another truck that would take them to the gold fields, they stopped at a bar. Cícero had a can of beer, and Júlio a Coca-Cola. Despite his uncle's criticism, he would not change the cold drink for a glass of beer. The hundred-mile journey to Serra Pelada was much more complicated than the trip from Imperatriz to Marabá. Cícero and Júlio were squeezed in among forty men on the back of the truck. All the would-be miners were seated with their legs drawn up so as to leave room for the knapsacks and saddlebags in the middle of the floor. There were young and old men, light-skinned and dark, speaking in a variety of accents. From their voices, Júlio realized that some of these adventurers searching for gold had left the states of Maranhão, Bahia, Mato Grosso, and Paraná. He was pleased that nobody asked him anything: he did not want to let slip that he was on his way to Serra Pelada to kill someone. And he was afraid of lying and saying he was a prospector because he might show that in fact he knew nothing about it. In order not to run that risk, he pretended to be asleep.

Júlio only opened his eyes when the truck started down a track through the rainforest and the jolting made the man to his left topple onto him. Júlio was impressed with what he could see around him. The track was so narrow that the sides of the vehicle were scraping the trees. You only had to stretch out your hand to touch a trunk, and if the truck slid at all it would end up in the middle of the undergrowth. In spite of this, the driver did not seem in the least bit concerned. He drove along at a speed Júlio considered far too fast in these circumstances.

This was the first time in his life that Júlio had been afraid of dying in a road accident. The torture lasted for twenty minutes until the track broadened and the truck pulled onto another dirt road. Almost an hour later, Júlio caught sight of an incredible scene. There were people everywhere. Not even in Imperatriz or Xambioá had he seen such confusion. The eighty thousand men living in Serra Pelada at the time seemed to fill every inch of the cindery earth. The truck came to a halt, and everyone got off quickly, jumping down from the back.

Not a single house was built of brick; all were made of wood. And all their roofs were black plastic or planks. Júlio was still staring with dismay at this pandemonium when he realized that the men who had made the journey with him had been stopped by policemen, who were searching them carefully and even opening their knapsacks and saddlebags.

No one could get into Serra Pelada without being checked by the police. This operation was intended to prevent weapons and alcohol from entering the gold field. Júlio remembered the revolvers he and his uncle had brought, hidden in Cícero's knapsack wrapped in socks. A policeman came up to him and patted his legs, stomach, back, and arms. Then he ordered him to open his knapsack. While Júlio was doing so, he looked back and saw his uncle being stopped by another policeman. If their weapons were discovered, there was bound to be trouble. The idea of being arrested in this godforsaken hole terrified him. He closed his eyes tight and prayed to the heavens for God to deliver them from this dilemma. When he opened his eyes again, he saw an extremely skinny man with a wrinkled face go up and shake hands with the policeman searching his uncle, smiling and congratulating him. Cícero was immediately able to avoid any search and having to open his knapsack. Júlio thought his prayers had been answered.

"Hi there, Armando," the man said to Cícero. "How was the journey?"

Júlio caught on at once that "Armando" was the pseudonym his uncle used in these parts. It was the name of Júlio's grandfather, Cícero's father.

"The same torture as always. But the main thing is we got here in one piece," Cícero replied.

"Is this the young guy you mentioned?" the man went on, jerking his chin in Júlio's direction.

"Yes, that's him. He's good."

"And what's your name, kid?" the man asked, extending his right hand toward Júlio.

"Jorge. My name is Jorge," he replied hoarsely, copying his uncle's idea of using his father's name.

"Good to meet you. You can call me Paraíba. My name is Daniel, but everyone calls me Paraíba. Let's go, the boss is waiting for you."

Paraíba's boss was someone known in the gold fields as Indio. Later on, Júlio learned that his real name was José Mariano, and that his nickname was no accident. He was born in an indigenous tribe in the Pará rainforest, and had been one of the first to arrive in Serra Pelada, back in November 1979. Nobody knew for sure, but the rumor in the muddy streets of the town was that in little more than two years of prospecting, Indio had amassed 200 kilograms of gold, which in those days was worth equivalent to around $3.6 million. He was dark-skinned, with well-defined features, small eyes, very straight black hair, a thin mustache, and a straggly beard that only partly covered his pointed chin. He was twenty-nine and like all the other prospectors lived in a wooden shack with a beaten earth floor and a plastic roof. Júlio would never have thought that someone looking the way he did and living in such a miserable shack could be so rich.

What everyone did know was that Indio had invested part of his golden fortune in cars and real estate. At a Volkswagen dealership in Marabá, he had acquired five cars, which he bought on sight for cash. The salesman who attended him told everyone that the prospector had taken the stack of money from a paper bag like the ones used for wrapping bread in. Indio had so much money that he used to travel to Marabá in a private plane at least three times a week to have fun with the girls there—no women were allowed into Serra Pelada itself. The flight lasted twenty minutes and cost at least 4,000 cruzeiros. Júlio did the calculations and realized that this man who looked so poor spent at least 12,000 cruzeiros a week just on going to Marabá. With all that money, Indio could easily pay more than 5,000 cruzeiros to get rid of an enemy. Júlio suggested to Cícero that they talk to the prospector and try to convince him to increase the price for the service, but his uncle took him to task, explaining that once a deal had been struck, money was never mentioned again with the client.

After they had lunch at Indio's place, Paraíba left with Júlio to point out the man he had to kill. They came to a huge crater, much wider than two soccer fields and some three hundred feet deep. Thousands of men covered in a gray, sticky mud were climbing out of this seemingly bottomless pit, carrying burlap sacks on their backs. There was a constant movement up and down the giant hole. The prospectors looked like ants as they swarmed up and down. This went on all day long: the men kept returning to the top of the crater along huge earthen ramps that snaked around the outside of the hole. Some had wooden ladders that were three feet wide and three hundred feet long so that they could reach the bottom. Paraíba told Júlio that one of these ladders had been baptized by the miners as "Goodbye Mom."

"What a funny name," said Júlio with a smile.

"The name might be funny, but the reason behind it isn't," Paraíba said.

"Why's that?"

"It's called that because every so often a guy falls off. And that means certain death, my boy."

"Seriously?"

"Of course, kid. Imagine someone falling down three hundred feet in this hellhole. At least two or three die like that every month."

Júlio knew at once what he had to do to kill this João Baiano without attracting anyone's attention. He would catch him when the miner was on this "Goodbye Mom" ladder and shoot him in the head. In the midst of all the noise and confusion, the shot would go unnoticed, and everybody would think that João Baiano had died from the fall. It would not be difficult. By the time it was discovered that the prospector had been killed by a bullet to the head, Júlio would be far away. The only problem was to find the guy. He and Paraíba had been at the edge of the crater for almost half an hour, and there was no sign of João Baiano. In fact, Júlio thought it must be impossible to distinguish anyone in this human anthill. Everyone looked alike, with sacks on their backs and their bodies covered with mud. Only occasionally was there someone who did not wear a hat. Yet Paraíba assured him that if he caught sight of João Baiano, he would recognize him.

They left the rim of the crater and walked around town to try to find him. As they went, Júlio wanted to know why Indio wanted to kill João Baiano. Paraíba explained he was one of nine men who worked for Indio. In return for a monthly wage of 10,000 cruzeiros (a little more than the minimum wage of the time), these men were meant to hand over everything they dug out to the boss. But when he discovered a nugget weighing 30 grams—which could be sold for 27,000 cruzeiros—João Baiano had tried to cheat Indio. He didn't tell anybody, but kept the gold for himself. However, one of Indio's employees found out and told their boss.

"But that's such a small amount compared to everything Indio has," Júlio said.

"It's not the money that's the problem."

"So what is?"

"The problem is that this kind of thing becomes common knowledge. Nobody says anything, but everybody knows what João Baiano did. If the boss did nothing, he would lose face. From that moment on, everyone working for him would think they can steal the gold and will start doing so. That's why you have to kill the guy. Understand?"

"Yes, I understand."

By now it was growing dark, and the men emerged from the pit to wash. There was no running water in any of the shacks, so they all washed together, in groups of twenty or thirty men, at standpipes coming from an artesian well. As they washed, a thick mud spread across the ground. The miners' faces and bodies gradually appeared as they were freed from this thick layer of dirt. Júlio couldn't understand how these men seemed so happy. While they were washing they sang, whistled, smiled at one another. It must be because they thought that one day they would strike it lucky, as Indio had done. Paraíba asked a man drying himself on his own shirt if he knew where João Baiano was.

"He left the mine earlier, straight after lunch. He said he had a stomach ache, and didn't come back," said the man, drying his hair all the while.

Júlio and Paraíba returned to Indio's shack as night fell, without having found João Baiano. As a result it was agreed Júlio would do the job that night. Despite never having seen the man he was there to kill, his uncle and Paraíba convinced him he would have no problem identifying him.

"João Baiano is a big, strong black man about five foot six. He's almost bald and has a gold tooth on the upper left side of his mouth," Paraíba said.

Júlio wrote this down in his notebook and read it several times until he'd learned the details by heart and had a clear picture of his victim. Paraíba told him he could find João Baiano at a snack bar close to the branch of the Caixa Econômica Federal bank, where the prospectors sold their gold.

"Baiano goes there every night to have something to eat and play dominoes," Paraíba said.

"So what do I do?" asked Júlio.

"Do your job, kid," Cícero butted in gruffly. "Since when do you need to be told what to do? Go there, find out who this guy is, and finish him off."

"Okay," said Júlio, glancing at his uncle, puzzled by the fact that Indio hadn't said a word. It was as if the person who had contracted him wasn't even there.

They all ate a supper of rice, beans, and dried meat. From a cooler, the prospector took out cans of Coca-Cola for his guests, and finally spoke, saying that he preferred to drink beer, but Major Curió—Sebastião Curió de Moura, a sort of mayor for Serra Pelada appointed by the then president João Baptista Figueiredo—had prohibited the consumption of alcoholic drinks in the town. Júlio was happy to have his favorite cool drink in such a hellishly hot place.

After the meal, Paraíba took him to the wooden hut that was the branch of the Caixa Econômica Federal, and pointed out the snack bar José Baiano was in the habit of visiting. Júlio sat down on the ground while Paraíba went over to the bar to see if Baiano was inside. He had not yet turned up, which was a good sign.

"I'm sure he'll be here before long," Paraíba said, then went on his way.

Júlio did not take his eyes off the bar. Four men were sitting on benches at a wooden table playing dominoes, while others stood around watching the game. There was a constant coming-and-going in the bar. Júlio was worried that João Baiano could enter without him spotting him. He himself was wearing a wide-brimmed straw hat to hide his face, and two shirts, one on top of the other. Following the crime, he would throw away the top one, which was black, and keep on the one underneath, which was white with blue stripes. While he was waiting for his victim to appear, he thought about how he was going to do his job. To kill him surrounded by so many people was a stupid idea. He would have to convince José Baiano to go with him to some solitary spot, and from what he had seen of Serra Pelada, the most convenient place was the crater where the prospectors dug for gold. This was about two hundred yards from the nearest shacks. At night, the hole was completely deserted. He could shoot the man, throw the body into the crater, and disappear into the darkness.

He grew tired of waiting and decided to go into the snack bar himself. Making sure the revolver was secure in his belt, he walked over to it. He went in and ordered a Coca-Cola. He took a long swig from the can and said he was looking for someone called João Baiano.

"Kid, there must be at least ten João Baianos here. I myself know three," said the man who sold him the drink.

"The one I'm looking for is a strong black guy, a bit younger than me, with a shaven head and a gold tooth," said Júlio, pulling down the hat to hide his face.

"Yes, I know who you mean. But he hasn't been in here today. Has anyone seen that big Baiano guy around here today?" the man shouted. No one replied.

Determined to find his victim, Júlio left the bar and began to ask everyone he came across in the street for João Baiano. Finally a white-haired old man not only said he knew the prospector, but could point him out to Júlio.

"He's that fellow over there, can you see him?" said the old man, pointing to a strong, almost bald black man who was walking away from them.

"Where?" asked Júlio.

"Over there. He's the one wearing the red cap and green shirt. Can you see him?"

"Yes I can. Thanks a lot," Júlio replied, setting off behind his victim.

He ran holding onto his hat with his left hand and the revolver butt at his waist with the other. When he was ten yards from João Baiano he stopped running and walked calmly along. He drew closer to him, controlling his breathing.

"Hey, friend. Are you João Baiano by any chance?" he asked, smiling at the man.

"That's me. Why do you ask?"

"I want to get a gold tooth and I was told that you know who can do that for me."

"That's easy, kid. There's a heap of dentists in Marabá who can fix it in no time."

"You've got a gold tooth, haven't you?"

"Not one. I've got three," said Baiano, opening his mouth to show his gold teeth. Two were on the lower jaw, one on each side. The third was the canine on the right-hand side of the top jaw.

This tooth was proof that Júlio had found the right man. He clearly remembered Paraíba telling him about the gold tooth João Baiano had in his upper jaw, on the right of his top set of teeth. Now all he had to do was kill him. To do that he needed first and foremost to get Baiano off this busy street where there were too many witnesses. Júlio told him he had just arrived in Serra Pelada and asked the prospector to show him around. Baiano said he had been on the go all day and wanted to return to his shack to rest. Júlio insisted, asking him to at least show him where the gold was found.

"The way I'm feeling, I'll fall asleep before I get there," said Baiano with a chuckle.

"Let's go. I at least wanted to see that spot. Then we can come back right away," Júlio insisted.

"No, I'm not going, kid. If you want, I'll take you there tomorrow, in daytime. But now I'm going straight home."

"Well at least show me how to get to the crater, and I'll go on alone."

"Fine. I'll take you near it."

As they walked along, Júlio and Baiano talked about the prospectors' routine. The best thing, the miner said, was the cinema. Every night at around eight, porno movies were shown on the screen put up in the middle of the street. As women were prohibited from entering Serra Pelada, there were usually as many as three thousand men in the audience. Júlio was curious to see this: he had not slept with a woman for two months now, and movies like that would be a treat.

On the corner of a poorly lit street where there were few passersby, Baiano took him by the left arm and said:

"All you have to do is go down here and turn into the second street on the right. Carry on to the end of that street, and you'll see the hole."

Júlio drew the revolver from his waistband and, hiding it under his shirt, thrust it at Baiano's stomach.

"If you open your mouth, I'll finish you off right here."

"What's this, kid?"

"Keep your mouth shut and take me to the hole."

"What are you doing?" asked Baiano, his voice quaking.

"If you take me there, I promise everything will be all right. But don't say another word. If you open your mouth again, I'll fill your belly with lead."

They walked some five or six hundred yards until they came to the rim of the crater. Júlio heard Baiano crying softly. For the first time, he looked closely at the face of the man he was about to kill. It seemed to him Baiano was much younger than he had imagined. His cheeks were still smooth, his face unlined, he had a long nose and big eyes. He asked how old he was, and Baiano said he had just turned nineteen. Just a kid, but Júlio was determined not to feel sorry for him. He had already killed people who were much younger. In 1978 he killed a thirteen-year-old boy—his youngest victim—on the orders of a big landowner in Paragominas, in Pará state, who wanted to force a couple who were slave workers to return to the ranch they had run away from. The boy was their son. If the man and his wife did not return to their slavery, the landowner was threatening to kill their other three children. With the same cool determination as when he'd fired a bullet into the head of that thirteen-year-old boy while he was playing soccer in the street, Júlio would end Baiano's life now. He told the prospector to take two steps forward toward the hole.

"Please don't kill me. I've done nothing," Baiano said two or three times, his voice choked with tears.

"Stay quiet, you bastard. I'm not going to kill you," said Júlio, taking off the black shirt and revealing the blue-striped white one underneath.

He ordered Baiano to walk to the edge of the crater and pushed the gun to within a handsbreadth of the side of his head. Then he pulled the trigger. The shot echoed around the hole as if a bomb had gone off. Júlio saw the prospector's body roll down the slope and ran off into the darkness.

He stuffed the black shirt down his trousers and threw the straw hat away. He only stopped running when he could feel his leg muscles aching with tiredness. He thought he had run about a mile. He was bathed in sweat, in the middle of nowhere. On one side was thick jungle. On the other shone the few lights of the town of Serra Pelada, which had electricity thanks to some diesel generators. He collapsed onto the muddy ground and waited until he felt rested.

He walked back to the town as if nothing had happened, but he was nervous, and his heart was beating fast. He was afraid someone might have seen him running away just after he shot José Baiano. Because of all the disputes over gold, Serra Pelada had more police than many of the big towns in the region. Júlio was very scared of being arrested. He was even more worried when he reached the town and realized he did not know where Indio's house was—he was meant to go there once he'd done the job. He did not want to ask anybody where the man who had hired him lived, as that might arouse suspicion. He spent fifteen or twenty minutes wandering lost along the dirt roads of the town, head down for fear someone might recognize him. He could not detect any unusual activity: apparently, the crime had not yet been discovered. He passed by the branch of the Caixa Econômica Federal, and suddenly knew where he was. Finding the route back to Indio's house would be easy.

When he arrived, he found his uncle Cícero, Paraíba, and

Indio talking animatedly outside the wooden shack. They were all sitting on benches with cigarettes in their mouths.

"Aha, here he comes at last!" said Cícero with a smile.

"Well, kid, have you done the job?" Paraíba asked.

"Yes, I have. I sent the bastard into hell," said Júlio, trying hard to seem glad about it.

"That's the way to do it," Cícero concluded, standing up to give his nephew a hug.

Indio said nothing, but picked up a bench and threw it at Júlio's feet, making him take a step backward to avoid it hitting him. He told him to sit down and tell them exactly how he had killed José Baiano. While he quenched his thirst with a can of Coca-Cola, Júlio described the episode in great detail, boasting about the clever way he had persuaded his victim to lead him to the edge of the crater.

"And Baiano's body is at the bottom of the hole?" Indio wanted to know.

"Yes. After I shot him, I saw his body fall into the hole and ran off as fast as I could," said Júlio.

Indio got up and started pacing up and down, running his hands nervously through his straight black hair. None of the others dared say anything. Júlio wanted to ask what the problem was, but thought it better to stay silent. The prospector moved about three yards from them and stood behind Cícero, Júlio, and Paraíba. Folding his arms across his chest and staring out into the forest, he said calmly:

"You're going to have to go down into the pit and get his body out of there."

"Now?" said Paraíba.

"No. In a month—of course I mean now, you idiot!" shouted Indio, without turning round.

"But why?" Júlio asked.

Indio turned to stare at them in a way that scared Júlio. He said that if João Baiano's body was left at the bottom of the crater it could cause him problems. It would be found the next day, with a bullet in the head, and Major Curió would definitely get the police to investigate who had killed him. Even though he thought any such investigation would go nowhere, Indio did not want to run the risk of having his name associated with the murder.

"That's why you three have to go there now, remove his body from the pit, and take it to a distant, isolated spot," he said.

"How are we going to do that, boss?" asked Paraíba.

"Take the pickup and put the body in it. Then drive to the river and throw it in," said Indio, taking the key to the Fiat 1000 from the pocket of his bermudas and handing it to Paraíba.

Cícero remained sitting on his bench, without saying a word. Júlio did not appreciate his uncle's lack of reaction: he didn't even offer to help recover the body. Five minutes later, he and Paraíba were parking the Fiat at the rim of the crater. They carefully descended into the pit, lit only by a flashlight Paraíba had brought. It was the first time Júlio had been there, at the heart of the biggest gold rush in the world. They descended in zigzag: the hole seemed bottomless. Some thirty feet from the bottom, Paraíba spotted a shape on the muddy ground. It was João Baiano's body. The corpse was facedown: the fall had caused injuries to the head and broken the right forearm. The head was covered in dark red blood that had soaked the mud around it.

Paraíba took the body by the hands, Júlio by the feet. They had only climbed some sixty feet when Baiano's broken arm snapped completely. The noise made Júlio drop the corpse in terror. He felt a stab of disgust. Frowning, he clamped his mouth shut and took a firmer grip. They continued their climb, with Paraíba lifting the body under the arms and clenching the flashlight between his teeth. The heat was almost unbearable, and so was their tiredness. Júlio could feel sweat pouring down his head, but did not want to wipe it away with a hand that was dirty from the mud and Baiano's dead body. When they reached sixteen feet from the top, Paraíba came to a halt to see if anyone was nearby. Everything was quiet. They sped up and threw the body into the pickup, then drove for thirty or forty minutes along a track through the middle of the rainforest until they came to the banks of the river Parauapebas. They took off their clothes and entered the warm water, still carrying Baiano's body. When the river was up to their waists, they let the body go, and the current carried it away. They took advantage of being there to bathe and get some rest.

When they arrived back at Indio's shack, they found the prospector on his own, stretched out in his hammock. Cícero had left to go kill one of his two victims.

"Your uncle will only be back tomorrow," said Indio. "You can sleep here or at Paraíba's place."

"I think I'll go and sleep at Paraíba's," Júlio replied.

The following morning, he was awakened by the sound of Indio kicking at the door of Paraíba's shack. Indio was in a rage. He was like a man possessed, his eyes popping out of his head. By the time Júlio had clambered out of his hammock, Paraíba was standing in front of his boss, his hands crossed behind his back and staring at the ground. Júlio went over to him.

"What kind of crap is this?" cried Indio through gritted teeth.

"I've no idea. It's impossible for that to have happened," Paraíba replied, without raising his head.

"What's happened?" Júlio wanted to know.

"You killed the wrong man, kid. That's what's happened," said Indio, shaking his head in disgust.

"That's not possible."

"Yes it is. The fact is, João Baiano is at work down in the crater, alive and kicking."

"Who says so?" asked Júlio.

"Nobody says so. I saw him with my own eyes!" shouted Indio, fists clenched and staring Júlio in the face. He went on, bellowing at him:

"A useless killer. That's what you are."

Júlio had never felt so humiliated. By now he had been a professional hitman for eight years, and had never had a problem of this kind. To be called a "useless killer" was the worst insult he had heard in his life. But he had to take it. Indio would not have said that João Baiano was still alive if he wasn't sure. Júlio raised his right hand to his mouth, unsure of what to say. Then, for the very first time, he made a gesture that was to stay with him for the rest of his life, like a nervous tic. Joining his thumb and index finger at the top of his nose, he slowly opened them as though he were combing his eyebrows. He repeated the movement time and again while he was thinking what he could do to sort out the problem. One thing was for certain: he had to kill the real João Baiano. He promised Indio that Baiano would not live to see another day. And he told him he would keep his promise without asking anything in return.

"You paid for me to kill João Baiano. And that's what I'm going to do," Júlio said.

"That's the least I expect. But be careful you don't kill some other poor guy by mistake," said Indio.

Júlio asked Paraíba to take him to the crater to point out exactly who the man was that he was supposed to kill. On the way there, he thought about what he had done the previous night. He had killed some poor man who had nothing to do with the gold stolen from Indio. Who was he? Did he have a wife and children? Probably not: he was very young for that. He had only just turned nineteen. Júlio had never been in a situation like this before. To kill somebody by mistake was terrible. The people who hired him always had some reason for wanting the death of their victims. But that kid he had murdered had not done anybody any harm. At least, as far as Júlio knew. He could not get used to the idea. He still could not understand where he had gone wrong. It was only when he talked to Paraíba that he discovered his error. The João Baiano he should have killed had a gold tooth on the left-hand side of his upper jaw. The gold tooth of the João Baiano he had murdered was on the right. Apart from that, the description of the two men was exactly the same: black, strong, almost five foot six, balding. Júlio realized his error at once. He had killed a man by mistake simply by not paying enough attention. A tremendous sadness gripped his heart. He was angry with himself. How could he have made such a stupid mistake? Indio was quite right to call him a "useless killer." But now he would use his sense of anger to eliminate the real João Baiano.

Paraíba pointed to a man in the middle of the crater who was climbing a wooden ladder with a sack on his back. "That's him," he said. Baiano's body was covered in dark gray mud. Even his face was smeared with it. Júlio did not want to repeat his mistake, so he waited for Baiano to reach the top of the crater and walked up to him. Using the excuse that he was looking for work, he started talking to the prospector. Their conversation did not last long. All Baiano said was that he had no idea who could offer him work, and continued on his way. But that was enough for Júlio to memorize his victim's features. He would recognize his face anywhere. After that, he bought four cheese sandwiches and two cans of Coca-Cola and spent the rest of the day near the rim of the crater. He didn't take his eyes off João Baiano, who went on working without realising he was being watched. When the work day was over, he washed at one of the standpipes in the street and then went home. Júlio followed some forty yards behind him. He saw where Baiano was living—a wooden shack with a plastic roof—and then returned to Paraíba's place. Night was falling. The door was open, but there was no one there. Júlio lay down in a hammock and tried to get some rest. It was only then that he remembered he had not asked God for forgiveness for having killed the wrong João Baiano. He stretched out in the hammock and prayed the ten Hail Marys and twenty Our Fathers. Now finally he would be able to sleep.

He woke up two hours later when Paraíba began to tug at the hammock.

"The boss wants to know if you've dealt with the guy."

"Not yet," replied Júlio, without getting up from the hammock, and closing his eyes once more.

"How can you be so calm, kid? How can you sleep if you haven't done the job?"

"Paraíba, it's all sorted out. You can tell your boss that I'll keep my promise to him. José Baiano won't live to see another day. I only need you to get me a really sharp knife."

"Yes, it's better to kill him with a knife," Paraíba agreed, guessing Júlio's intentions.

"Why?"

"Because bringing a revolver into Serra Pelada is prohibited. If Baiano's body appeared with gunshot wounds, the police would make a great effort to find out how it happened. Stabbings are more common."

"So how come my uncle got in carrying two revolvers, if they are prohibited?"

"I'd already arranged everything with the head of the guards carrying out the searches. When you arrived, I gave him a bit of money and your uncle entered without being checked."

"I get it," said Júlio, and then went back to sleep, complaining he had a headache. Before doing so, however, he asked Paraíba to wake him at one in the morning.

He woke ready for action. He washed his face in a bucket of water kept at the back of the hut, put on two shirts—a black one over a white one—and borrowed a cap from Paraíba. He picked up a handful of manioc meal with egg he saw in a pan, and then went out to do another night's work. He knew exactly what he wanted to do. He was so certain of his plan he didn't even bother to take his revolver. All he carried was the knife—as long as his forearm—which he stuck in the waistband of his US Top jeans. The blade was so long he found it hard to walk properly, and limped along as if he had a damaged right leg. The streets of the town were deserted. So much the better: he did not have to worry about being seen by someone. The only thing bothering him at that moment was having to wear two shirts in the unbearable heat.

When he reached João Baiano's shack, Júlio could not believe what he saw. It couldn't be easier. The miner was asleep outside in a hammock. Júlio pretended he was just passing by. He walked on another fifty yards, then turned around, scanning the street with his eyes. Not a soul in sight. He came to a halt, a couple of feet from João Baiano. The miner was snoring like a pig. His mouth was wide open as he lay on his back with his arms folded across his chest. Júlio took a good look at his face. He didn't want to run the risk of killing another person by mistake. This time there could be no doubt: this guy was the same one Paraíba had pointed out in the hole. But just to be safe, Júlio wanted to see the gold tooth on the left of his upper jaw. He bent down, resting his hands on his knees, and leaned over the hammock. Then all he had to do was to thrust his face toward Baiano's mouth. He saw the gold tooth. On the left side. He pulled out his knife, and was about to slit his victim's throat when he remembered one of the rules he had learned from his uncle: never kill a sleeping person.

He didn't know what to do. Should he wake the man up to kill him? That seemed ridiculous. Baiano would be bound to try to react. He might even shout out, and arouse the attention of the people living in the nearby shacks. Júlio took off his black shirt and wrapped it around his left hand. He lifted one foot over the hammock, so that the miner's body lay between his legs. In a single movement, he sat on Baiano's chest and stuffed the shirt in his mouth so that he could not make a sound. The miner woke up terrified, his eyes wide open. He struggled to get up, but it was impossible. He only calmed down when Júlio slid the knife across his throat and told him not to move.

"Because of you I killed a poor innocent guy," he said.

Baiano groaned and shook his head, as if begging not to be killed.

"Because of you, I was called a useless killer," said Júlio, and pressed the knife across Baiano's throat. Blood spurted onto his chest and drenched his hands. The bleeding went on and on. If Júlio had known it would be like this, he would have thrust the knife into his stomach, as he had done with Amarelo, the first man he ever killed. Taking the hammock down from its hooks, he wrapped the body in it; then, trying not to make any noise, he dragged it inside the hut. He left it in a corner on the left side of the room. He bolted the door from the inside and climbed out of the window, making sure he shut it before he left. He felt strangely happy. Proud of himself. Nobody would call him a useless killer ever again. He was so pleased with what he had just done that he forgot to pray for forgiveness.

A day later, he and his uncle returned to Imperatriz. Baiano's body was only discovered three days later—according to Cícero, because of the foul smell coming from his shack. Since there was no evidence about the perpetrator, João Baiano was buried as a suicide.

IT WAS ONLY as he recalled this episode sitting on the sofa in his house that Júlio Santana realized the name João Baiano represented not one but two deaths in his notebook. This was important for the calculation he was making. Every page he turned brought back the memory of other crimes he had committed. Men, women, and even children whose lives he had taken for money. The children were a small minority: he had only killed four people aged under sixteen. Fifty-nine of his victims were women. Most of these deaths were contracted by their husbands, who accused them of betraying them. When Júlio finished adding up the number of murders he had committed, he discovered he had killed 424 men. In total, he was responsible for 487 deaths, without counting the three people he had killed before 1974, the year he began to write down the details in his notebook.

He took another good look round his house, and wondered if it had been worth killing so many people. He no longer lived in a riverbank village as he had in his childhood. Now he was in the center of Porto Franco. The town was very different now from the one where he grew up and lived until he was eighteen. At the start of the 1970s, Porto Franco had about 1,500 inhabitants. By April 2006, this had grown to eighteen thousand. Most of the streets were still beaten earth, but the main ones had been asphalted. He lived in much better conditions than when he was a boy. But he had not become rich, as he had thought would happen when he decided to become a professional hitman.

He leafed through the pages of the notebook until he came to one that was marked with a big "X" in the top right-hand corner. He knew exactly what that meant. It was the sign of the break between him and his uncle Cícero. That "X" symbolized the end of a friendship he had believed was eternal. And all because of accursed money.

To the left of the "X" he read:

KILL NATIVO DE NATIVIDADE [PRESIDENT OF THE RURAL WORKERS' UNION] IN CARMO DO RIO VERDE, GOIÁS STATE. CONTRACTED BY MAYOR ROBERTO PASCOAL. TRAVEL ON OCTOBER 22. CONTACT IN THE TOWN GENĒSIO. FEE: TWO MILLION CRUZEIROS.

THE YEAR WAS 1985. Júlio was already married and had left Cícero's house in Imperatriz a year earlier to reside with his wife in Porto Franco. But there was still a strong bond between him and his uncle. In addition to their family ties, they still worked together. Cícero was the one who passed on the jobs to Júlio. His uncle was a kind of intermediary between the people contracting the killings and him. Hardly a month went by without them shooting someone. Sometimes, Júlio took part in the murder of several persons at the same time, such as when he led the slaughter of six farmers in the town of Pimenta Bueno, in Rondônia, in June 1987.

Júlio's wife loathed Cícero. She said he was the one responsible for her husband taking up the appalling life of a professional killer. Júlio always protested, saying that it had been his own choice. He had wanted to earn money and to have great adventures. His uncle had done no more than help him do what he wanted to do. This argument always took place when Cícero came to the house to pass on a contract to his nephew. And this was what had happened on that Wednesday, October 16, 1985. As usual when they needed to talk about work, Júlio and his uncle walked a mile to the banks of the river Tocantins. It took Cícero less than ten minutes to pass the details on to his nephew. He was to kill Nativo da Natividade, president of the Rural Workers' Union in Carmo do Rio Verde, in the interior of Goiás state. The person contracting them was the city mayor, Roberto Pascoal, who said he was incensed at the political influence Nativo had in the region, and especially by the rumors that the trade unionist was going to stand as a candidate in the 1988 municipal elections. When he contacted Cícero, Roberto Pascoal said he wanted to get rid of Nativo before he became even stronger and more prominent.

Everything had been arranged. Júlio was to take a plane from Imperatriz to Brasília on the morning of October 22, a Tuesday. At the airport in the federal capital, a man called Genésio would be waiting for him, and would take him by car to Carmo do Rio Verde, about a hundred miles away. Once there, he would have all the time he thought necessary to end Nativo Natividade's life. He would be paid two million cruzeiros for the service (a little more than three times the minimum salary at the time, which was 600,000 cruzeiros). Júlio thought that did not seem very much, and wanted more money. But his uncle said he had already tried to bargain with the mayor and that was the most he could get.

"Besides, earning two million for a couple of days' work isn't bad at all. There are people who don't earn that for a whole month's work," said Cícero, repeating what he always said when his nephew complained about the amount he was going to receive for a contract.

The trip from Imperatriz to Brasília was much easier than Júlio had imagined. This was the first time he had been in a plane. When he saw the Amazon rainforest from high in the air, the nerves he had felt during the takeoff soon gave way to enormous fascination. The river Tocantins winding through the rainforest and the vast world of trees were the most beautiful things he had ever seen. From the sky, the houses of Imperatriz looked like toys. Pressing his face against the window, Júlio remembered the happy, peaceful childhood he had known there. A time when all he did was swim in the muddy waters of the Tocantins, roam through the jungle, and kill animals so that his family could eat. That was a proper life. Not this one, killing people. But by now he was thirty-one, and did not know how to do anything else.

When he got off the plane in Brasília, he saw a light-skinned man about five feet seven and with graying hair, who was holding up a piece of paper on which was written "Jorge": as he had done in Serra Pelada, Júlio used his father's name as a pseudonym. He presented himself to the man, who confirmed he was the Genésio that Cícero had mentioned. They got into Genésio's car—a red Belina—and set off for Carmo do Rio Verde. The journey took six hours, including a stopover at a roadside restaurant for lunch. Genésio did not say much. On the rare occasion he did, he said he thought it was unnecessary for the mayor to have brought a hitman from Maranhão state to kill Nativo.

"I could have done the job myself," Genésio said over their meal.

"So why didn't you?" Júlio asked.

"The mayor said it was safer to bring a killer in from outside, so as not to raise suspicions about him."

"I think that's true."

"That may be so, but I could have done with that money you earned for killing Nativo."

"I haven't been paid anything yet."

"What do you mean? The mayor told me he had paid up front."

"That's right. But the person he paid is the friend I work with. I'll only get the money when I return to Imperatriz."

They reached Carmo do Rio Verde at around five in the afternoon, and went straight to Genésio's house because he wanted to rest after the journey. Júlio said he had no time to waste and that he would like to see where Nativo lived and where the Union of Rural Workers' headquarters was. Genésio said he didn't have to worry, everything had been arranged. Half an hour later, a blue VW Beetle pulled up outside the house. The driver was a skinny young black man, who introduced himself to Júlio as "Pelé." They went to the union building and saw Nativo's beige Beetle parked in the road outside. Nativo's house was about a mile away. Júlio learnt from Pelé that he was thirty-three, married and the father of two small children. He was very quiet, and only left his house to go to the Union or to farmers' meetings. Thanks to this information, Júlio concluded that the best moment to kill the trade unionist would be when he was returning home from work. He would shoot Nativo just as he pulled the car up in front of his house. And he wanted to do it that same night.

He and Pelé returned to Genésio's house. Genésio told him his return trip had already been planned. After killing Nativo, Júlio would be taken back to Brasília in a municipal ambulance, and from there he could catch the first bus to Imperatriz. Before Júlio could ask why, Genésio said he would have to return by bus because the mayor wanted to save money. Júlio turned down his offer to have supper, arguing that he needed to be outside Nativo's house before he returned from work. Pel'e dropped him there and drove off. Júlio sat on the ground and waited, about fifty yards from his victim's house.

It was almost seven in the evening by the time the trade unionist's car came around the corner. Júlio adjusted the straw hat to hide his face and got to his feet. He walked slowly on the far side of the street toward Nativo's house. He pulled the revolver from his waistband at the same moment the car came to a halt. Júlio was about twenty yards from him, but he wanted to get closer, to make sure of the shot to the head. The trade unionist seemed relaxed. He had no idea he was on the brink of death.

Nativo walked slowly toward the front door. From a distance of ten yards on the other side of the street, Júlio leveled his revolver at him. He was about to pull the trigger when he saw a little girl aged five or six open the door and run laughing to her father. Júlio didn't have the heart to kill a man in front of his own daughter, so he immediately lowered the gun to the ground. The trade unionist bent down and picked up the little girl. Júlio saw them kissing each other before they went inside the house.

Determined to kill Nativo that night, Júlio spent more than an hour outside his house, hoping he would come out again. But nothing happened. He walked all the way back to Genésio's house, and told him what had happened.

"But tomorrow I'll kill the guy, no matter what. You can bet on that," he assured him.

He spent the whole of that Wednesday October 23, 1985 in the blue Beetle beside Pelé, trailing Nativo da Navidade. At eight thirty in the morning, he left the house and went straight to the headquarters of the Union of Rural Workers of Carmo do Rio Verde. He did not reappear even for lunch. He went home at six twenty that evening. This time, Júlio couldn't finish him off because there was a group of kids playing soccer in the street, and he didn't want any witnesses to his crime. Pelé parked the car at the corner. Júlio's idea was to wait until the kids had finished and then knock on Nativo's door. The instant Nativo appeared, he would shoot him in the head. The soccer game was soon over, but the boys stayed in the street, sitting directly opposite the trade unionist's house. This was becoming far more complicated than Júlio had first thought. As he stroked his eyebrows with the thumb and index finger of his right hand, he wondered how long he would have to wait before the gang of kids went their way.

Pelé opened a pack of crackers they'd bought to stave off their hunger. Before Júlio could put the first one in his mouth, Nativo came out of his house carrying a briefcase, and got into his car. They followed his Beetle at a distance of a hundred yards, without switching on their lights. Five minutes later, the car pulled up outside the union building. The street was deserted. Now was the moment. Júlio put on the straw hat, took the revolver out of his waistband, and jumped out of Pelé's Beetle. In his haste, the hat fell off.

Damn it! It'll have to be without it! thought Júlio.

He reached Nativo's car before the trade unionist got out of it. He pointed his gun at the man's head, but Nativo reacted at once. He seized Júlio's right arm in both hands. In the struggle, Júlio pulled the trigger four times—the autopsy showed that there were three bullet holes to the chest and one in the neck. He only finished firing when he was certain Nativo was dead. (In 1996, eleven years after this episode, the mayor Roberto Pascoal was tried as the man behind the crime, but acquitted.) Júlio looked up and down the street but could not see anyone. Pelé had already brought his car alongside him. Before Júlio got in, he even had time to run and pick up his straw hat. Pelé was terrified.

"God in heaven! What dreadful thing have you done?"

"What do you mean, kid? Didn't you know I was going to kill the guy?" replied Júlio.

"Yes, I did. But I've never seen anything like that, right in front of my eyes."

"There's a first time for everything in life," Júlio said, and told Pelé to drive back to Genésio's house.

Fifteen minutes later, the municipal ambulance arrived to take

Júlio to Brasília. It was as they were saying goodbye that Genésio said something that led Júlio to split from his uncle Cícero forever.

"God be with you, kid. You did a great job."

"Thank you, Genésio."

"I think I agree now with the mayor. You were worth the six million cruzeiros he paid for the service."

"Six million?" said Júlio with a smile, thinking Genésio must be joking.

"Isn't that what you got?"

"I wish I had. I was only paid two million."

"What's that, kid? Are you lying to me? I was the one who negotiated everything with the mayor. He paid six million for Nativo's death."

"Are you sure, Genésio?"

"Of course. I think someone is making easy money behind your back."

"You could be right."

"Well anyway, get into the ambulance as quickly as you can, before they find the body of that bastard and things get hot around here."

Júlio was so disturbed at the idea that his uncle was defrauding him that he felt angry the whole way back from Carmo do Rio Verde to Brasília. He did not want to believe it. If Cícero had behaved like that over Nativo, then he must have acted the same way with all the contracts he had passed on to him. Júlio could even understand that his uncle should receive some money for the murders, because he was the one who dealt directly with the people giving the orders. But that had to be done in an open, trustworthy fashion, without any lies. And what sense did it make for him to run all the risks, to have the weight of so many deaths on his conscience, if Cícero was going to keep most of the money? If they had split it fifty-fifty, that would still not be fair. Worse still, if what Genésio had just told him was true, he would receive two million, whereas his uncle would keep four million. He was even more offended when he recalled having told his uncle that he thought this amount was not very fair for killing a president of a farming workers' union—in the hitmen's list of prices, killing an influential trade unionist is one of most expensive contracts. But Cícero had told him that was the price, end of story. Júlio wanted to confront his uncle as quickly as possible to throw all this in his face.

HE ONLY REACHED Imperatriz twenty-four hours after leaving Brasília. On that Friday morning, he went straight from the bus station to his uncle's house. He found him sprawled on his sofa, watching television.

"Didn't you go to the barracks today, Uncle?" he asked.

"No. I'm having a day off."

"You're always doing that."

"What's this? Why are you looking at me like that?" said Cícero, not getting up from the sofa.

"I always thought you were my friend."

"What are you saying, Julão?"

"I thought you liked me, and that I could trust you."

Cícero sat up and asked what had happened. Júlio said he had learned that his uncle had been lying, and kept the larger share of the money from the contracts he fulfilled. Cícero vehemently denied this. He said he loved his nephew like his own son and would never cheat him, much less for money. Yet Júlio was sure it was all lies.

"It would be much better if you at least told me the truth and apologized."

"Listen to the way you're talking to me!" said Cícero reprovingly.

"Bullshit! You're completely worthless, Uncle. Worthless!"

"Julão—"

"You heard me. You got me into this dreadful life as a killer, and still you cheated on me, keeping the money for the work I did."

"You'd better leave now, before I do something I might regret," said Cícero, getting to his feet, his eyes open wide.

"Do what? Kill me? I don't believe you have the guts," said Júlio, thrusting his chest in the face of his uncle, who was several inches shorter than him.

"You're lucky my revolver isn't in my belt."

"Well, mine is," said Júlio, pulling his gun out of his trousers and pushing it into Cícero's face.

He had never seen such a look of fear in his uncle. He had gone pale, and was shaking like a green sugarcane stalk. For the first time in his life, Júlio was tempted to kill someone without being paid for it. In his heart he felt only bitter hatred. His teeth were clenched and he was breathing heavily. He only realized he was crying when he felt the tears wetting his lips. He didn't want to admit it, but he was very sad. Above all, he wished that none of this had happened. If his uncle had not been such a damned liar, everything would be different.

"Put down that weapon, Julão," said Cícero in a calm, almost gentle voice.

"Don't worry, Uncle. I'm not going to kill you. Even though you deserve a bullet in that shameless face of yours."

"Put the gun down, my son."

"I'm not your son. God save me from anything as terrible as that. The only reason I'm not going to kill you is because you're the brother of my father, may God keep him." (Seu Jorge had died in 1983 at the age of fifty-three.)

With that, Júlio lowered his revolver, turned on his heel, and walked out. His teeth were still clamped, and he was breathing heavily through his nose.

"Have you stopped to think that you owe me everything? If it weren't for me, you would have nothing, Julão! You would be nobody," Cícero shouted from inside the house. This enraged Júlio. Still in tears, he hurried back inside the room. Tucking the gun in his belt, he pushed his uncle back down onto the sofa with both hands.

"What a shit life you gave me. I'm an assassin, Uncle. I make a living killing people. And you have the nerve to say that's a good thing?" he shouted.

Cícero said nothing, with the same expression of fear on his pallid face that Júlio had seen when he first confronted him.

"I understand now why there are people who kill others out of hatred. I'd love to finish you off right now. The only reason I don't do so is my father. But get one thing into your head . . ." said Júlio, waving his finger in his uncle's face. "If I ever see you again, I will kill you. Have you got that? Whatever day, hour, or place it is. I'll kill you like a dog."

Júlio ran out blindly into the streets of Imperatriz. He was sobbing from anger and sadness. He was almost sorry he hadn't killed Cícero. He had already murdered so many people he did not know and who perhaps did not deserve to die. For the first time in his life, he wanted to kill someone on his own account.

He should have done it, but he did not want to burden his father's soul.

He only saw his uncle again eight years later, in 1993, at his burial. Júlio went to the cemetery out of regard for the friendship he and his uncle had known when he was a boy. Cícero had died at the age of fifty-three of lung cancer due to a lifetime of smoking. The funeral was attended only by his two wives, his five children, and half a dozen friends. Júlio knew just one of them: Sergeant Santos, from the military police, who lived and worked in Imperatriz.

Júlio was surprised there weren't more people from the military police present at the funeral. But talking with Sergeant Santos, he learned that Cícero had never been part of the force. The story that he was a military policeman was simply another lie his uncle told to hide the fact that he was a contract killer. He had bought the uniform he wore when he wanted to keep up appearances from Sergeant Santos. Now Júlio understood why he had never seen Cícero at work. When he saw his uncle in the coffin, looking far thinner and frailer than when he had last been with him, he felt sorry for him. But he would never forgive him. He went on his way before the coffin was covered with sand.

He is still in tears whenever he remembers the argument he had with Cícero and what made him break with him. He would have given anything for none of that to have occurred, to have been able to rest in his own home undisturbed by those memories. He was still remembering all this when he was interrupted by his wife and daughter, who had come back from the church. He was lying on the sofa, his hands folded across the notebook on his chest, open at the page marked with an "X." He pretended to be asleep. His daughter came over, kissed him on the cheek, and tried to prize the book from him. He took hold of her hands and opened his eyes. They smiled at each other, but Júlio's wife noticed there was something wrong. She said his eyes were red, and asked if he had been crying. As he did not like lying to his wife, his smiled without saying anything, got up, and shut himself in his room. He put the notebook back in the old knapsack and hid it behind the wardrobe. He decided he would never pick it up again. From that Sunday, April 16, 2006, he would write down the contracts he accepted on any scrap of paper that came to hand. But he would never touch that notebook again. The 487 deaths recorded there were enough.

The Killer's Repose

THE ALARM ON Júlio's cell phone went off at exactly two in the morning. His wife woke up in a fright. What on earth was her husband going to do at that time of night? She was used to him getting up in the early hours when he went out to kill someone. But this time she knew that could not be the case. It was August 2006, and two months earlier Júlio had promised he would never murder anyone again. She was sure he wouldn't lie. Not to her. His wife was the only person who knew what Júlio did for a living. She told her daughters, and the few neighbors with whom she had any contact, that he was a military policeman. Like his uncle Cícero, he had learned to use the uniform, which he got from his uncle himself, to camouflage his real activity. But that morning he was not leaving home to kill anyone. The alarm at two in the morning had a very different purpose.

At the age of fifty-two, Júlio said he was exhausted by that appalling life of killing one person here, another there. In addition, he no longer had the agility, the strength, or the sharp sight he had once possessed. As he grew older, working as a killer became increasingly tough. He had decided to rest, to change not only towns but states in Brazil. In order not to attract the attention of their neighbors, he wanted to leave Porto Franco, the town he came from in Maranhão, in the early hours. His wife and children knew the move was to be that Saturday. What they had not realized was that they would have to wake up at two in the morning to climb into the truck of one of Júlio's friends. Against the wishes of his wife, who wanted to leave nothing in the house, the family was going to take only a few bags filled with clothes, the twenty-inch TV set, the sound system, and the DVD player. All the furniture was to stay in the house, which had been sold by Júlio to his truck-driver friend for 15,000 reis, to be paid off in ten installments of 1,500 reis. He sold his car (a Fiat 127) to another man he knew, and the canoe for 8,000 reis in cash.

Before giving the canoe to its new owner, Júlio did something that unburdened his heart. On the morning before the move, he found the knapsack where he kept the notebook with the list of all the contract killings he had done, got into the canoe, and traveled almost half an hour until he reached a completely isolated stretch of the river Tocantins. He took with him the .38 revolver he had used to kill close to five hundred people. When he arrived, he removed the gun from his waistband and threw it into the bag. In it, as well as the revolver and the notebook with the list of his victims, were two stones the size of coconuts he had put there just before he got on board. In the middle of the river, he closed his eyes and thanked God for delivering him from the life he had led. Then he tossed the bag into the Tocantins and watched until he saw it sink in the muddy waters. He knew that in this part of the river it was more than thirty feet deep. The revolver and the notebook would never torment him again. He felt lighter, maybe even a little happy. He couldn't wait to return home and tell his wife what he had done. He was sure she would be proud of him for doing so.

His wife's influence was essential in Júlio's decision to leave Porto Franco and move to another state. Ever since the day her husband told her he was a hired killer (in February 1985, eleven months after they were married), she never stopped pleading with him to leave behind this dog's life. But Júlio always argued that it was the only thing he knew how to do, and that it was thanks to that wretched profession that he was able to support his home and children. He had earned everything he possessed by killing people wherever he was contracted to do so.

The longest journey he had ever made to carry out a contract had occurred in 1989, when he went to Paraná state to kill a businessman's brother. The crime was paid for by the businessman himself, because he wanted to keep the share of an inheritance that belonged by right to his youngest brother. Now, though, that kind of event would be forgotten forever. Júlio could finally live in peace with his wife and children, whom he told he had retired from the military police and planned to take them to a much better place than Porto Franco.

"Is there a movie house there, Dad?" his eighteen-year-old son asked.

"Not in the town where we're going to live. But close by there's a bigger city, with a movie house, a shopping mall, all those things you like," Júlio replied, as he lifted the TV into the truck.

During the ride from Porto Franco to Palmas, the capital of Tocantins state, he sat next to the window, with his wife on his left. The children were sitting on the bunk behind the driver and never stopped talking because they were so excited at leaving the town they were born in for the first time in their lives.

At that time of morning, the streets of Porto Franco were completely empty. When they left their house behind, Júlio asked the driver to take the road that ran alongside the river Tocantins. He wanted to see one last time the landscape that had always been part of his life, in the good times and the bad. It was in this river that, exactly thirty-five years earlier, he had killed his first victim, the fisherman Amarelo, in August 1971. It was also on the river Tocantins that he had his first sexual encounter, with Ritinha, in 1972. It was here too that he had played with his two brothers, Pedro and Paulo. They now lived in São Luis, the capital of Maranhão state; he occasionally spoke with them on the phone. It was also on the banks of this river that he grew up watching his mother, Dona Marina (who by now was seventy-three years old, and lived with Paulo in São Luis) as she washed their clothes and dealt with the animals and fish the family ate.

The full moon of those early hours lit up the rainforest and cast a bluish tinge on the water. Júlio wished he could spend all his life in Porto Franco, and yet he knew he would never manage to stop working as a killer if he did not leave the town. On Christmas 2004 he had promised his wife he would give up his life as a killer, but the constant offers of work had prevented him from doing so. In March 2005 he had turned down two contracts, but had not been able to resist an offer of 3,000 reis from a landowner in the town of Dom Eliseo in Pará state who wanted to be free of a son-in-law who beat up his daughter. Known for his discretion and efficiency, not a month went by without Júlio receiving at least one phone call from someone interested in his services. He couldn't retire if he went on living in Porto Franco. Nor would his marriage last if he carried on as a hired gun.

ON HIS FIFTY-FIRST birthday—June 23, 2005—his wife had said, in tears, that she would not spend another year married to an assassin. Either he gave up that life or he could forget her and their children. Even though his wife's insistence upset him, he knew she was right. What he hated most of all was when she started to say that if he did not stop killing people, he would go to Hell. Ever since she had begun to attend the Assembly of God church, his wife repeatedly told him that his ruse of saying ten Hail Marys and twenty Our Fathers, which Júlio continued to do after every murder, was not proper repentance. She said that God would only forgive him if he truly repented. One such conversation took place early one hot morning in July 2005, when they were both lying in bed.

"But I am repentant," said Júlio.

"If you were, you would never do it again. Besides, one of the Ten Commandments in the Bible is 'Thou shalt not kill,'" she said.

"I know that very well."

"You know it, but you don't respect it."

"It's my job, woman. What do you want me to do?"

"I want you to give up that terrible profession and start a new life. I'm warning you. If you carry on with it, I'm leaving and taking the children with me," his wife said, her voice choked with sobs, but with a determination that made Júlio admire her even more. The only woman he respected more than his wife was his own mother. He thought his wife was always right, even when she contradicted him. Or especially then. In twenty-two years of marriage, he had never raised his voice at her. And when his wife was angry at him, he said nothing, but sat there, head down, barely listening. He always used to say that she was his safe haven. He could commit all kinds of atrocity out in the street, but he knew that once he returned home, he would find her waiting for him, always ready to offer him comfort, however upset she was with her husband's way of life.

He wouldn't know how to exist without her, the mother of his two children and a wonderful companion. As they drove along that early morning in 2006, Júlio cast a glance at her. She seemed relieved, at peace. He recalled all the anguish his profession had brought her. All those sleepless nights, worried if her husband would come home alive.

That first part of the trip, from Porto Franco to Palmas, was only the start of a journey that would change the life of their family forever. Putting his arm around his wife's shoulders, Júlio remembered the first time he had seen her.

IT WAS NOVEMBER 1983, and Júlio had been hired by a moneylender in Teresina, in Piaui state, to kill a bank clerk who owed him money. He was to receive 550,000 cruzeiros for the hit, the equivalent of almost ten times the minimum salary at the time, which was 57,120 cruzeiros. When he arrived in the capital of Piaui, one of the moneylender's employees was waiting at the bus station for him. The man, who identified himself as Sergio, drove him in a brown Dodge Caravan to the bank where the victim worked. The name of the person Júlio had to kill was Adilson.

"The boss lent that sonofabitch a million and a half, and he hasn't paid any of it back yet. The debt is increasing all the time because of the interest, and the guy says he's never going to manage to pay it off," said Sergio, while they were waiting for Adilson to come out of the bank.

"That sounds complicated," said Júlio, who wasn't paying much attention.

"That's not the half of it. I myself have tried to collect the debt three or four times, but Adilson always finds an excuse not to pay."

"So what does he say?"

"That he has no dough . . . that he has to pay the rent, his bills, his children's schooling . . . and he's been spouting that crap for five months now."

"But wouldn't it be better for your boss to force him to pay rather than to kill him? If he dies, your chief is never going to see the color of that money."

"You don't understand. The boss is sure that Adilson is never going to be able to pay the debt off. And as he lives from lending money to others, he needs to show people what happens to anyone who asks him for money and doesn't pay. If he allows Adilson to go around unpunished, everyone who has borrowed money from my boss will think that if they stop paying nothing will happen."

"I get it. You just have to show me who he is, and I'll give him his one-way ticket before the day is out," Júlio guaranteed him.

At ten minutes past four on that hot Friday afternoon, Adilson left the bank. He was wearing jeans and a long-sleeved blue shirt tucked in at the waist. He was thin, probably around five foot four, and looked about thirty-five or forty years old. Dark-skinned, he had black curly hair, but no beard or mustache. He walked approximately a hundred yards from the door of the bank to the bus stop. Five stops later he got off outside a supermarket. Júlio got out of the Dodge to follow Adilson home, keeping a distance of thirty yards between them. Sergio protested that there was no need for him to follow his victim.

"I know where Adilson lives, Jorge," he said, using the pseudonym Júlio adopted whenever he was carrying out a contract.

"I know that. But I want to see where it is."

"Why, for the love of God?"

"To see what the house is like, and if the street is busy or not ... that kind of thing."

"All right."

"Wait here."

Fifteen minutes later, Júlio was back. Adilson's street was quiet, not asphalted, and with only dim lighting from two streetlamps, one on each corner. Júlio's plan was to kill his victim in the same way he'd done many times before. He would knock on Adilson's front door, and when the bank clerk appeared, he would shoot him in the head. In order to get away from the scene of the crime as quickly as possible, he told Sergio he would need a motorbike.

"I've got one, but I can't lend it to you," said Sergio.

"Why? Isn't it any good?"

"It's not that. The thing is, I always ride it around town. If after you've killed Adilson someone notices the license plate, I'll be the one to pay."

"That's nonsense, Sergio. We only have to take the plate off. I've done it more often than you can imagine."

"Seriously?"

"Of course. Trust me. Everything will be fine."

After eating yams with chicken at Sergio's house, Júlio took his motorbike and went out to do another night's work. He arrived at Adilson's house a little after eight. There was no one in the street. He left the motorbike locked, kept the helmet on, and banged three times on the front door. He kept his right hand holding the revolver hidden behind his back. When he heard the door open, he got ready to kill another poor guy. He would only shoot once, straight at the head. But it was a young boy about ten years old who came to the door. He had curly hair and very dark eyes. The boy said his father had just gone out.

"If you hurry, you'll be able to catch up with him," he said.

Júlio ran his hand through the boy's hair and went back to the motorbike. He felt dreadful at the thought of depriving the child of the chance to grow up with his father. He started to wonder whether Adilson had other children, if he loved his wife, if he had any brothers or sisters. It was for this and other reasons that he always avoided meeting any of his victims' relatives or friends. It was all much easier when the person he had to kill was no more than a name and a face. That was how he would treat Adilson: as a name to be erased. He didn't want to know if the bank clerk was a good father or husband. He was there to kill him. And that was what he was going to do. He went off to find him. When he caught up with Adilson, he was sitting on the curb at the bus stop. Júlio couldn't manage to kill him there and then because before he could draw near, Adilson boarded a bus that had just arrived. Júlio followed it on the motorbike until the bank clerk got off again. It was impossible to kill him there either. It was a busy street, and his victim was walking on the sidewalk together with other people.

Júlio did not take his eyes off him, until he saw him enter a bar. He waited exactly ten minutes before he went inside as well, carrying the helmet under his left arm. He could feel the revolver butt rubbing against his navel. Before sitting down, he scanned the bar with the same acute eyesight he had once relied on when hunting in the Amazonian jungle. There were only ten wooden tables in the bar, with wooden chairs scattered around the bare cement floor. To the right of the entrance was a counter about thirteen feet long, with a cash register, a glass cabinet containing croquettes and pies, and a few glasses with beer dregs in them. Opposite the till was a jukebox where customers could choose the song they wanted to hear. There were two people behind the bar: a fat old man with graying hair, stubble, and eyes that looked as if they were being squeezed by the enormous dark lines underneath, and a girl who looked sad but was very pretty. Júlio could never have imagined that this young woman with straight black hair was to become his wife and the mother of his children. He pushed between two men sitting on stools near the bar and ordered a can of Coca-Cola and a glass with ice. From close up, he could see the waitress was even more beautiful. She was wearing a cotton dress with her hair hanging loose and wore no makeup. She had strong features, a square face with a wide mouth and thin lips. Her light-colored eyes contrasted with her smooth, dark skin. Her dainty nose looked as if it had been handmade. Júlio wanted to ask her name, but did not have the courage. And also because he was not there looking for a woman: he had a job to do. He examined the bar again and saw that Adilson was still sitting on his own at a table next to the counter. He was drinking one beer after another. Within twenty minutes, the bank clerk had already drunk two cans, and asked for a third.

Júlio divided his attention between the man he had to kill and the woman he wanted to get to know. He didn't like the rude way that the other customers spoke to her behind the counter. Some of them called her "my little black girl," others "cutie." One of them was even ruder, saying she was "hot stuff."

Júlio really wanted to rebuke them for talking this way, but knew that would only complicate things. He had never gotten involved in a fight in a bar, and this was not going to be the first time. Forcing himself to stay calm, he asked for a chicken pie. When the waitress served it on a plastic plate, he made sure he looked her in the eye. She responded with a half-smile. At that very instant, Júlio decided he would not leave Teresina without at least finding out her name.

Before that, though, he had to put an end to the life of Adilson, who was still sitting alone at the same table. By now he was drinking his fifth can of beer. He seemed to be crying as he did so. He would take a swig, then rest his head on his hands, arms on the table. He was talking to himself. Two or three drunks tried to engage Júlio in conversation, but he paid them no attention. He ordered another Coca-Cola and glass of ice.

"You're not from here, are you?" the waitress asked as she put his drink on the bar.

"No," he replied, not knowing what else to say, surprised that the girl had spoken to him.

"I knew you weren't. I've never seen you around here. Where are you from?"

"From Marabá," he lied.

"I've heard of it. It's in Pará state, isn't it?" she went on, wiping the counter with a filthy cloth and avoiding looking at Júlio.

"That's right."

"They say lots of people are killed there over land disputes."

"That's right."

"It seems you're not one for much conversation."

"The thing is, I'm a bit preoccupied."

"What with?"

"With my work."

"And what's that?"

"I'm a military policeman," replied Júlio after a few moments' hesitation.

"So what's happened with your job to make you so preoccupied?"

"I think it's better if I don't talk about it now."

"Fine. Sorry for interfering," said the waitress, returning to her tasks.

Time passed by and Adilson showed no sign of leaving the place. On his table were six beer cans and an empty glass. The bar was starting to empty when the bank clerk stood up and walked toward the toilet, which was five or six yards to the left of where Júlio was sitting. Adilson even brushed against him, and apologized. It was already past one o'clock in the morning, and Júlio was anxious to get the job done as quickly as possible. It was only then that he could approach the waitress behind the bar. He was watching her wash up half a dozen glasses in a sink behind the counter when he saw Adilson come out of the toilet. The bank clerk was staring straight at him. Júlio looked away, but noticed that the man was heading in his direction. He glanced back at him, and was sure that Adilson wanted to come up and talk. It occurred to him that perhaps his victim knew who he was and would kill him before he was shot himself. He could have gone into the toilet to check his own gun.

While these thoughts were going through Júlio's mind, Adilson drew closer and closer. Júlio was sure the man was aiming for him. Without getting up, Júlio stuck his right hand under his shirt and clasped the butt of the revolver. He was determined, if necessary, to kill the bank clerk right there, in the middle of the bar. In front of everyone, even the pretty waitress. In another two steps Adilson would be standing right in front of him. Júlio pulled his revolver out from his waistband, but still kept it covered by his shirt. When he was only three feet away, Adilson halted and spread his arms wide, as if he was expecting a shot in the chest. Júlio couldn't understand a thing. All of a sudden, Adilson began to shout:

"Flamengo are the world champions! World champions!" he roared, and gave Júlio a big hug.

It was only then that Júlio understood what was going on. He was wearing a shirt from Flamengo, his favorite soccer club, with the number 10 and the name Zico on the back. The title Adilson was shouting to the four corners of the earth—world champion!—had been won by the Rio de Janeiro team two years earlier, in 1981. Even so, Adilson was celebrating as if it had just happened. It must be the beer talking, thought Júlio. The bank clerk was still hugging him and insisting he join him at his table. Júlio tried to escape any way he could. He didn't want to be seen talking to the man he was supposed to kill. But Adilson, completely drunk, would not let him go. In the end, Júlio went over to his table. They chatted for more than half an hour. The first ten minutes were entirely about soccer. Adilson said there was no team like that 1981 Flamengo one, with Zico, Júnior, Adílio, and Nunes the biggest stars.

As well as the World Club championship, Flamengo won the Brazilian championship in 1980, 1982, and that year, 1983.

"But there's no one like Zico," said the man.

"That's true," replied Júlio sincerely.

From soccer, Adilson abruptly changed topics. Forgetting Flamengo, he began to talk about the problems that had brought him to the bar. His wife hated it when he arrived home stinking of beer. Besides that, she always said that a man who owed money to God and to the whole world should not waste it drinking cachaça. He was only there that night because he had had a row with her. They had quarreled over a rumor going around the town where they lived that a moneylender Adilson owed money to had hired someone to kill him.

"I said she shouldn't worry about that. I told her it was nonsense, but she didn't listen to me and is desperate," he said.

"Okay," said Júlio, glancing down at the empty glass on the table.

"So we argued and I left home to come and drink. When I get back, we'll argue again. She says I should use the money I spend on drink to pay off that sonofabitch moneylender."

"So why don't you do that?"

"Do you think the few cents I spend at the bar is enough to pay off my debt? It isn't, kid. It's a lot of money," said Adilson, with a strange smile on his face.

"How are you going to manage to pay him then?"

"It's simple. I'm not going to pay anything. I'm not in any position to pay. Not even if I were to shit gold," said the other man, still smiling nervously.

"But you owe him money."

"I know, my friend," he said, grasping Júlio's forearm with his right hand. "But there's nothing I can do. The debt has increased so much, there's no way I can settle it. Even though I'd like to pay that bastard and free myself from this hell. But I know I can't."

Júlio was weary of hearing this talk. He hated having heard all that: he didn't need to know about Adilson's problems. He didn't even know why he had been so interested in that poor jerk's story. He was there to kill him, and that was what he was going to do. Shortly before two in the morning, he said he had to be going and persuaded the bank clerk to accompany him. He said he had a motorbike and could give him a lift. He walked out of the bar with Adilson practically hanging onto his left shoulder. In the doorway, he turned back to the counter and nodded to the waitress. From five or six yards away, she could not take her eyes off him. "I'll be back," he said in a low voice, trying to make sure she could read his lips. From the smile he received in return, he thought she had understood the message.

As soon as they began to walk along the street, Adilson wanted to know where Júlio's motorbike was. He asked the same question three times. Júlio gave the same answer each time: "Just near here." He'd left the bike parked in the street behind the bar. He was so concerned about completing his task as soon as possible in order to go back and talk to the waitress that he'd forgotten the helmet on the counter.

Completely drunk, Adilson would not stop singing the Flamengo anthem.

"Once with Flamengo, always with Flamengo. I'll always be with Flamengo . . ." he chanted in a loud voice.

Júlio was worried that this chanting would wake people up and make his job more difficult. At that time in the morning, the streets were completely deserted. There was total silence, apart from the bank clerk's slurred voice. Three blocks farther on, Júlio judged he was far enough away from the bar to kill his victim without the shot being heard by the waitress he wanted to get to know. He stretched his right hand out toward his revolver, but then decided to walk on a little farther. With the whole neighborhood asleep, the sound of the gunshot might reach the bar, and he did not want that. They walked on another three blocks. The heat of the night and the weight of Adilson, who was still leaning on his shoulder, left Júlio bathed in sweat. The clerk was so drunk he did not realize he was being led nowhere. He kept on chanting:

"We're going to win. To win! Flamengo till I die."

Júlio looked all around him, in front and behind. No one was about. He pulled the revolver from his waistband and, still walking, pressed the barrel against Adilson's head, three inches above his right ear. At the moment he pulled the trigger, he turned his head away. He heard a strange noise, like a stone hitting a piece of tin stuck on a wall. It was the bullet burying itself in his victim's skull. He saw Adilson fall to the ground like a sack of flour. Blood was pouring from his head. Júlio examined his own clothes, and saw there was some blood on his left shoulder and arm. He pulled off his red and black shirt and used the underside to clean himself. The street was still deserted. Apparently the shot had not woken anyone up. He dragged Adilson's body over and propped it up against the wall of a house, then went back to the bar along another street. However much he tried, he could not stop whistling the Flamengo anthem.

Júlio would never forget the smile the waitress gave him when she saw him come back into the bar. He noticed a genuine pleasure and unexpected warmth in her. By now it was half past two in the morning, and the place was empty, apart from a man who was fast asleep with his arms and head on the table. The old man who had apparently been in charge was no longer there. Júlio asked if he could still get a drink, and when she said he could, ordered another Coca-Cola and a glass of ice.

"Don't you drink alcohol?" she wanted to know.

"Only occasionally. But I've been crazy about Coca-Cola ever since I was a boy."

They introduced themselves and stayed talking while she cleaned the cement floor with a wet cloth. She complained that every day was the same drudgery. She spent the night serving rough men and on top of that had to clean the bar before she could go to sleep. She told him the old man Júlio had asked her about was her grandfather, her mother's father, and that he was a good man. He was the only one who had offered to help her six years earlier when her mother died of tuberculosis in Belém, in the state of Pará. Her father had vanished before she learned to speak. Her mother made ends meet by working as a maid in family houses in the capital of Pará. She was seventeen when she was orphaned.

"And how old are you now?" asked Júlio.

"Twenty-three. And you?"

"Twenty-nine."

Júlio couldn't understand how he could be so struck by a woman he had only just met, and immediately feel concern about her. Yet he was already sure he would do anything he could to make her happy. He wanted to take her hand, to embrace her, kiss her, but he didn't have the courage. He thought that listening to some music might help him overcome his shyness. He asked if he could buy a token to put into the jukebox. The waitress told him that he could, but that he didn't need to pay. He went over to the box with its flashing colored lights, searching for the ideal song. When he saw "I'm Going to Get You Out of Here," by Odair José, he knew that was the perfect music for the occasion. "This is for you," he said. She smiled her thanks at him, but did not stop wiping the floor. When it came to the refrain, Júlio went over to her and sang softly:

"I'm going to get you out of here. I'm going to take you to stay with me. And I don't care what the others may think."

"You're crazy," she said, with a wry smile.

"No I'm not. I'm being serious. I'm leaving here tomorrow. Come with me."

"You must be sick. We've only just met."

"I know. But I want you to go with me now. I want to make you happy."

'Forget it. What a crazy idea.'

This made Júlio feel incredibly sad. He knew that this young woman was right. It really made no sense wanting her to go away with him when they had only just met. And yet he was certain that was what he wanted. Although he was disheartened, he went on talking to her. The way in which she spoke of her grandfather, her mother, of her wish to have her own house and family, only made him all the more convinced that he wanted her as his wife. Not simply to have sex or fun with her. But for her to be the mother of his children. Day was already breaking, and they were still talking, seated at one of the tables. Júlio said he had to leave, because he needed to catch the bus at the station at six thirty. He took her hands in his and asked if he could kiss her. She said nothing, but closed her eyes. It was a quick, nervous kiss, but one he would never forget. They kissed each other again three or four times. With each kiss, Júlio was increasingly sure that he wanted this young woman to be his wife. He was about to leave the bar when she called him back.

"If you really want to take me with you, come in here again. Then we can talk more and you can meet my grandfather," she said, staring into his eyes.

"That's what I'll do. You can be sure of it," he said, and they exchanged another kiss.

Júlio made another five journeys to Teresina to spend more

time with her and to gain her grandfather's confidence. The last two times, he appeared wearing the military police uniform his uncle Cícero had bought him. He thought the uniform was a great help. With her grandfather's approval, they were married legally (at the grandfather's insistence) in March 1984. There was no celebration. On their wedding day, Júlio was twenty-nine years old and she was twenty-four.

NOW, TWENTY-TWO years later, he, his wife, and their two children were leaving Porto Franco, where they had lived ever since they were married, to start a new life in another state. Júlio thought he could finally offer his wife the happiness he had promised her the day they met. Enough sadness. Like the sadness he had caused her the day when, giving way to the suspicions she kept voicing about his work, he decided to tell her that he was a professional killer. This was eleven months after they had married. Afterward, she spent days sobbing, lost weight, and fell ill. She refused to eat, and would not let her husband touch her. She said she would not sleep with a murderer and the only reason she did not leave the house was that she was pregnant with their first baby (who died aged nineteen in 2004) and did not want the child to go through the same ordeal as she had faced, having to grow up without a father. She was so frail and said that she was not going to be able to nourish herself and the fetus. She only began to eat again after a doctor told her that she ran the risk of losing the baby.

Following his confession, it took years for the relationship with her husband to improve. And it never returned to what it had been at the start, when she was always happy and affectionate. She loved seeing him come back from work wearing his military police uniform and then stretching out beside her on the bed. To discover all this was a lie and that the man she'd married was a killer was too heavy a blow for her. She lost count of the number of nights she pretended to be asleep when she heard her husband opening the front door. She curled up in bed whenever Júlio tried to touch her. Often he gave up, left the bedroom, and went to sleep on the sofa. But he never forced her to do anything she did not want to do. And she never stopped saying that she loved him. She always told him that she couldn't understand how someone so loving toward his wife and children could kill people. And worse still, for money. "It's my job, woman. It's my job," he replied each time, so calmly she was left even more stunned.

Despite all that she suffered, his wife never left him. Whenever Júlio came home with a troubled face, she did all she could to please her husband even if she herself was very upset. She knew he was feeling bad because of some dreadful act he had committed. She hated it, but felt she had to give her husband strength. However absurd and terrible his work might be, he was the father of her children. Júlio usually said nothing, just sat on a chair in the kitchen while his wife stood and stroked his head, hugging him to her. On one of the rare occasions when he did talk, he said hoarsely: "Today I killed a fourteen-year-old kid."

This was the only time during their twenty-two years of marriage that Júlio told his wife about a contract he had undertaken. He never told anyone else about them either. Not even those paying for the crimes, or the intermediaries. However much he was praised for his experience, discretion, and efficiency, he never felt proud about being a killer. Nor did he ever wish to know for what reasons the persons hiring him wanted someone dead. Curiously, however, without exception those paying for his services seemed to want to tell him their motives. It seemed to him as if they were trying to justify their deadly wish.

ONE OF THE MOST frequent questions he heard from people who hired him was if he had ever been convicted. Not once. That at least he was proud of. And however much his wife warned him about the risk of getting caught, Júlio always repeated what he'd heard his uncle say so often: "Out here in the interior, the cops don't get involved with gunmen."

This was until one day in May 1987, when he found himself handcuffed to the bars of the cell in the police station at Tocantinópolis, in Tocantins state. He had been caught trying to escape after killing a woman who had murdered her own eight-month-old child to get revenge on her husband, who was cheating on her. Horrified at the death of the baby, the husband was the one who hired Júlio.

That day, Júlio had left his house in Porto Franco toward the end of the afternoon on the red Honda 125 motorbike he'd bought four months earlier. It was easy to reach Tocantinópolis: it was a town on the opposite side of the river Tocantins from Porto Franco.

Júlio drove down to the riverside a mile from his house, parked the bike under a tree, and boarded one of the canoes that ferried goods and passengers across the Tocantins. In less than a minute, he was on the other side. He'd already arranged everything with the trader Luciano (aged thirty-four) who had hired him. Luciano had told his wife that he was bringing a friend to lunch at home. During the meal, he would go out to buy beer in a nearby bar and leave his wife alone with his friend: Júlio Santana. A quarter of an hour later, Luciano would return, and find his wife dead. No one could ever accuse him of the murder. He had witnesses at the bar who could testify that he was not at home at the time. For the plan to succeed, Júlio simply had to get back to Porto Franco without being stopped or seen by anyone.

"Don't worry, I can guarantee a good job," he told Luciano.

To the few people who knew him in Tocantinópolis, Júlio was a military policeman. He intended to use this in his favor. He arrived at the town wearing his uniform. Underneath it, he had on a pair of bermudas and a black T-shirt. He also stuffed a big straw hat under the shirt so that he could take it out when he was getting away, in order to hide his face. After the crime, he would remove the uniform and put it into a plastic bag. He would leave Luciano's house by the front door, as if nothing had happened, and pedal off on a bicycle left against the wall for him. He would reach the riverbank in no more than two or three minutes, and board another canoe. Then he would cross the river, pick up his motorbike, and soon be back home, safe and sound. He had already been paid 5,000 cruzados for the contract (equivalent to a little more than three times the minimum wage at the time, which was 1,641 cruzados).

Everything was going as he and Luciano had planned. Until, that is, the trader announced he was going out to buy beer. At that precise moment, his wife (Alzimara, aged twenty-nine) went into the bathroom. Time was passing, but she did not reemerge. Júlio counted five minutes on his digital watch and then went over to the bathroom door. He could not hear anything: she must have guessed what was about to happen. Júlio asked if he could get some water from the fridge. Alzimara shouted that he could. He grew nervous: what had at first seemed like an easy job was becoming a lot more difficult than he could have imagined. He went to the back of the house and saw the plastic barrel where he was supposed to kill Alzimara. Luciano had insisted on this: he wanted his wife to be drowned. "That was how she killed our baby," he told Júlio when he hired him. The barrel was full to the brim. But Alzimara showed no sign of coming out of the bathroom. Seven minutes had gone by, and Júlio couldn't wait any longer. He barged into the door with his right shoulder, knocking it down. She was crouching between the toilet and the wall of garish tiles.

"Please don't kill me," she whispered.

"Why do you think I'm going to kill you?"

"Because ever since I did that dreadful thing to my child my husband says he's going to send someone to do the same to me."

"And why do you think I'm the one who's going to do it?"

"Because you're from the police and have got a gun. Please don't kill me. Have mercy on me."

Without another word, Júlio took the woman by the left forearm and dragged her out of the bathroom. Alzimara clung on to anything she could find: the toilet bowl, the pipes of the sink, the bucket of dirty washing on the floor. And she kept shouting:

"Help! For the love of God, someone help me!"

"If you're not quiet, it'll be the worse for you."

"Help! Help!" she kept on shouting.

To make her shut up, Júlio punched her in the face. Alzimara passed out. This was the first time ever that Júlio had hit a woman. He had already killed several of them, but to hit a woman seemed to him like the act of a coward. In the circumstances, though, he could see no alternative. He managed to drag Alzimara to the back of the house. He plunged her head into the barrel until the water reached her breasts. Twenty or thirty seconds later, she came around. She struggled with all her might, kicking her legs in all directions and holding onto Júlio's arms with a desperate strength. He kept his hands around her throat even though she was scratching his arms with her fingernails.

He was determined not to let go until she had stopped moving, but suddenly changed his mind when a scene he'd witnessed fifteen years before flashed through his head. He was in the same position as the men who had tortured José Genoino (the man he thought was called Geraldo) back in 1972, in the Araguaia rainforest. Of all the tortures suffered by the person who in those days was a guerrilla fighter, that simulated drowning seemed to him the worst. Júlio would not do something like that. He had never approved of torture. Apart from anything else, that was not his job. He was a killer by profession, not a torturer.

Stretching out his right hand, he took a blue towel hanging on the clothesline a couple of feet from his shoulder. He pulled Alzimara out of the barrel, took out his revolver, and wrapped it in the towel to muffle the sound of the shot. While Alzimara was still trying to get her breath back, he shot her in the head. Then he pushed her body back into the barrel up to the waist, and went back inside the house.

Luciano had still not reappeared. Júlio took off the uniform, stowed it in the plastic bag, then prepared to leave the house wearing the clothes he had on underneath, and with the straw hat on his head. But as he opened the front door, he saw two men and a woman standing in the doorway.

"What was all that shouting in here?" asked the woman, a plump lady who appeared to be about sixty years old.

"No, there was nothing like that in here," Júlio answered.

"What do you mean, nothing? We heard Alzimara shouting for help," said one of the men.

"That wasn't here. There's been no argument here. I'm a friend of Luciano's."

"Where is he?" asked the same man, a short, strong-looking black man about five foot two.

"He's inside. If you like, you can come in and see," said Júlio, and walked calmly over to his bike.

"That's a lie! We saw Luciano leave, and he hasn't come back yet," said the woman.

"You must all be crazy. Now, if you'll allow me, I need to be on my way," said Júlio, mounting the bicycle.

"Hold onto him! Hold him and I'll go and see if Alzimara is all right," the woman said to the two men, who immediately gripped Júlio by the arms.

Two or three minutes later, a terrified cry could be heard.

"My God, that sonofabitch has killed the poor woman," she howled.

Júlio tried in vain to free himself from the two men who were pinioning him. Before he was led away to the police station, he saw Luciano hiding behind a lamppost at the corner of the street. Júlio could not believe that after committing crimes in towns and cities all over Brazil, he had been arrested here in Tocantinópolis, only three miles from his own house.

At the police station, Júlio was handcuffed with his arms behind his back and made to sit on a wooden chair. Opposite him on the far side of the table sat the police chief, Estevão Gomes, a thin man with a shaven head, dark eyes, and a long nose. He sent a policeman to accompany the two men who'd

brought Júlio to the station back to the victim's house and began
to interrogate the prisoner. Júlio said nothing, apart from that
he was innocent and had done nothing. The plastic bag Júlio
was carrying when he was caught lay on the table between the
two men.

"What's this?" asked the police chief in a sharp, aggressive
tone.

"My things."

"Are you from the military police?"

"Yes, sir."

"So why on earth did you kill that woman?"

"I didn't kill anyone, your honor. I've told you that several
times already."

"So who did kill that poor woman?"

"I have no idea."

"Listen to me. While you were in that house, the neighbors
heard the woman shouting for help. Shortly afterward, you
came out, covered in sweat, and the woman was found dead.
And there was no one else in the house. What do you expect me
to think?"

"You can think whatever you like. But I didn't kill anyone."

"What a joker! We'll see if you think it's so funny after you've
spent a few days in the cell," the police chief said. Then with the
help of another policeman he pushed Júlio into the cell, leaving
him standing there, his hands cuffed to the bars in front of him.

From there, Júlio could hear the sound of the typewriter keys
as the clerk took down the testimony of the woman who was
accusing him of the murder. The police chief repeated everything she said so that the clerk could draw up the incident
report. A little less than an hour later, the policeman who'd gone

to Luciano and Alzimara's house returned to the station and said that the man's wife really had been murdered, by a bullet to the head.

"What about the poor woman's husband?" the police chief asked.

"Some neighbors saw him leave the house, but he still hasn't returned," the policeman answered.

In the early hours of the following morning, for the first time in his life, Júlio Santana was tortured. Still handcuffed to the bars of the cell, he was kicked, punched, and beaten by the police chief and the two other policemen. One punch, launched by one of the men he could not identify, split his top lip, leaving him with the sour taste of blood in his mouth. Estevão Gomes kept saying that if he confessed to the crime, the beating would stop. But Júlio continued to say he was innocent. He was ready to die before he confessed to killing that woman. The punishment only came to an end as day was breaking.

"We'll be back later to continue our little conversation," said the chief with a sarcastic smile.

Júlio wanted to reply, insisting he had nothing to say, but did not have the strength. His ribs and stomach were burning with pain. The cut on his mouth would not stop bleeding. He was so tired his legs had gone numb—he had been standing up for almost twelve hours—and his whole body was aching from the beating he had taken. In this state, he thought he must be dreaming when he heard his wife's voice. He was only half awake, with his eyes closed and his elbows resting on the bars of the cell, his head in his hands, but he could recognize that voice anywhere and in any circumstances. He could hear his wife talking to the police chief, but could not make out what they were saying. He found it very odd that she should be chatting with that guy. He struggled to call out her name as loudly as possible. There was no reply. He shouted another two or three times, until a policeman came to the cell and told him to be quiet.

"After she's talked to the chief, your wife will come and see you," said the cop.

"I want to see my wife now!" Júlio insisted.

"Since when do you reckon you give the orders here? If you keep on causing trouble, the chief will send your wife away without you getting to speak to her. So just stay quiet."

Júlio felt like the lowest of the low when he saw his wife approach the cell. He could think of no worse humiliation than to have his wife see him in this condition. A prisoner, beaten up, with his clothes torn. They talked for less than ten minutes. She told him that she had learned of his arrest from the same man who had hired him. Following Júlio's capture, Luciano had gone to their home and told his wife everything. Among other things, he had said that the police chief was well known for accepting bribes to release criminals from jail. Since the case was a very serious one—a homicide—they would need something worth a great deal to persuade the chief to let him go. It was Luciano's idea that they should offer him Júlio's motorbike to pay for his freedom. In the conversation she had just had with the police chief, his wife had handed him the bike keys and papers, in return for a promise that her husband would be back home that evening.

"Are you crazy, woman?" Júlio shouted angrily.

"You make a living killing people, and I'm the crazy one?" she replied.

"That sonofabitch is going to keep the motorbike and never let me out of here. Those bandit cops are going to kill me in jail."

"That's not going to happen."

"How do you know?"

"You think I'm stupid, don't you? The stupid one in our family is you, Júlio, for getting into messes like this. Just look at the situation you've put us in."

"I want to know how come you're so sure the chief is going to order them to release me."

"Before I gave him the motorbike key, I asked for a guarantee. He gave me the incident report," she said, pulling the sheet of paper out of the bermudas she was wearing.

"So what?"

"The chief said that this report is the only document with any evidence against you. Without the official report, they have nothing on you. And since you're going to escape, no one will be able to link the death of that poor woman you killed to you. Got it?"

"That's true. But I'm not sure it'll work out."

His wife continued, saying that Júlio would also have in his favor the testimony that Luciano was going to give, in which he would swear that Júlio was in fact his friend, and would never kill Alzimara. This was the best way the trader could think of to avoid any suspicion of he himself being involved in the death of his wife. If Júlio remained in jail, it was highly likely that Luciano would also be arrested.

"All right. So when can I get out of here?" Júlio asked his wife.

"The chief said that at noon on the dot he and the two cops will go out to have lunch. He is going to leave the door to the cell and the station open. The bag with your military police uniform and your gun will be under his desk. All you have to do is put the uniform on and get out of this hell."

"That sounds easy enough. What about my motorbike?"

"Forget it, Júlio. You don't have a motorbike anymore. I'm going home now. When you get there, we'll have a proper talk about all this."

"I'm so sorry you had to go through this shame," he said, avoiding looking at her.

"This to me is nothing. The greatest shame in my life is being married to a murderer."

Júlio only raised his head when the sound of his wife's slippers on the cement floor of the police station died away. He caught a last glimpse of her shadow on the wall. He didn't know what was worse: to stay in jail with his aching body, or to return home where he was bound to feel even more humiliated. And yet he knew his wife was right.

Everything turned out exactly as she'd said. At noon, the police chief himself opened the cell door, unlocked the handcuffs and then left with the two policemen. Shortly afterward, Júlio was walking calmly along the dusty streets of Tocantinópolis. Reaching the riverbank, he boarded a canoe, which left him on the other side, in Porto Franco. His motorbike was where he had left it, parked under a mango tree. But now the red Honda 125 he'd bought only four months earlier was no longer his. Better to lose his bike than his freedom.

HE WOULD NEVER forget that Tuesday, May 12, 1987. When he reached home only twenty minutes after leaving the police station in Tocantinópolis, he was greeted by his wife, who did not say a word. As he took a shower, his sides ached when they came into contact with the water. His mouth was still bleeding. He put on a pair of shorts and sat on the toilet, stroking his eyebrows with the thumb and index finger of his right hand as he tried to pluck up the courage to face his wife.

He left the bathroom and went to lie down on their bed. His wife came in soon after, carrying a cloth and an aluminum bowl full of hot water. She cleaned her husband's wounds, making him howl in pain, and put a dressing on his top lip. Still she said nothing, apart from that she loved him very much, but that she did not know how much longer she could put up with living this terrible life as the wife of a professional killer. In return, he told her that he loved her too, and that he would never again let his work interfere with their life as a couple—by now they had been married three years and two months.

"You don't understand, do you? Can't you see that a dreadful profession like yours is bound to get mixed up in our lives?" she said. She was crying, and her hands were trembling.

"But it's my job."

"Júlio, listen carefully to what I'm going to say. Either you find other work or one day I'll leave you."

"You're right. I promise I'll do everything I can to stop doing these jobs and start something else. I only need you to give me time."

That night, they slept in each other's arms. Júlio felt protected in his wife's embrace: it was as if nothing dreadful could happen. All the weight of the deaths he had caused seemed to disappear when she held him like that. Not for anything did he want to lose her. But it took him took him another nineteen years to fulfill the promise to give up his profession as a killer so as to live at peace with his family. It only became a reality that morning in August 2006, when Júlio, his wife, and two children left Porto Franco in a truck. Two months later, in the town of Carolina in

Maranhão state, he shot his last victim. This was a public official whose death was contracted by his own son. The youngster,
aged twenty-four, paid Júlio 900 reis to kill his father, arguing
that he came home drunk every day and beat his wife.

When Júlio returned home in the early hours after committing the crime, his mind was made up not to kill anyone else for
the rest of his life. After taking a shower, he lay down next to
his wife, put his right arm around her back, and whispered: "It's
over." There was no answer.

He only realized that his wife had heard him over breakfast
that morning, when she asked if she could really believe what
he'd said in bed. Júlio swore that he would never kill again, and
the couple had a relaxed, even animated conversation the likes
of which they had not enjoyed in years. They began to draw up
plans for the future. They would buy a plot of land in some town
or other in another state in Brazil's interior, and would make a
living from farming and from the clothes she would sew and
sell. Their new house would have to be close to a bigger city of at
least two hundred thousand inhabitants, so that their children
could have access to good schools and the things they liked:
shopping malls, parties, and the movies. All this seemed too
good to be true to Júlio's wife, who only really believed what he
had promised one day in mid-August in the same year, when he
came home and said he'd bought the land.

On the property was a spacious house of 1,300 square feet,
with three bedrooms, a large kitchen, two bathrooms (one
outside), and a terrace where they could put up at least four
hammocks. It had piped water and electricity. Only a quarter
mile away was a stream whose clean waters would be ideal
for the children to have fun in. The former owner had planted

manioc, rice, millet, tomatoes, and lettuces. Júlio intended to cultivate the same things. The property also contained several mango, guava, breadfruit, and carambola trees, as well as some chickens and pigs.

After spending thirty-five years killing people all over Brazil, Júlio thought this would be the ideal place to live out his life at peace, with his family. He was so at ease with himself that he slept during the journey from Porto Franco to Palmas in a friend's truck, early one morning in August 2006.

Júlio, his wife, and two children spent the next day, a stiflingly hot Sunday, in the capital of Tocantins state. They caught a bus that left at seven thirty that evening for Brasília. During the twelve-hour journey, his wife and children were so happy that Júlio was convinced he was doing the right thing. They continued on from the federal capital to the region where they intended to live, and reached it as night was falling on a hot Tuesday. They were all really pleased and satisfied when they saw their new house—Júlio had already visited there when he bought it. That night, he and his wife made love in a way they had not done for years. Without the barrier of the fact that he was a hired killer placed between them, everything was going to be different. Better.

The next morning, stretched out in a hammock on the terrace, he watched his wife sweeping the tiled floor and the children playing in the shade of the trees. He pushed hard against the wall with his left foot and swayed to and fro, his arms folded across his chest.

This was the first time in his life that he felt truly happy since that afternoon of August 7, 1971, when at the age of seventeen he had killed the fisherman Amarelo. Now, aged fifty-two, he could lead a proper life, without the ordeal of having to kill some poor person here, another one there, just to pay the bills and put food on the table. His children would never know they had a father with such a dreadful past. He hoped that over time, his wife would also gradually forget all the horrors he had committed. And God would surely not refuse him forgiveness. He was determined that nothing would lead him to kill again. No one in their new location knew about his past, and so would not offer him that kind of contract. Even if they did, the answer would be no. Not for all the money in the world would he ever rob someone of their life. He did not need any more money. He already had all he needed to be happy: a good house, his farming, and his family. And he had even managed to keep some of what he had earned as savings.

Nowadays, Júlio Santana is in the habit of saying that the only thing preventing him from living completely at peace is when every so often one or another of his victims appears to him in dreams. The last time this happened—on September 6, 2006, he woke up in a sweat in the early hours. He ran his hands through his wet hair and went to lie down in one of the hammocks out on the terrace. In his nightmare, he had seen the bloody face of the miner João Baiano, the nineteen-year-old he'd killed by mistake in Serra Pelada back in 1982. Júlio says he believes he still has this kind of dream because he has not been completely forgiven for all the crimes he has committed. Whenever this happens, he recites the ten Hail Marys and twenty Our Fathers that, as his uncle Cícero taught him, should guarantee his forgiveness.

Then he goes back to sleep.

Born in 1969, KLESTER CAVALCANTI is considered one of the greatest Brazilian investigative journalists. He worked for many years with the leading news magazine in Brazil, *Veja*. His books, *Viúvas da terra* (2004), *The Name of Death* (2006), and *Days of Hell in Syria* (2012), have each won him the prestigious Jabuti literature prize in Brazil. They explore and denounce problems in contemporary Brazil, and range from condemnation of the deforestation of the Amazon to the biography of a Brazilian woman who has devoted her life to freeing thousands of Brazilians from modern-day slavery. Other awards include Best Environmental Report from South America, the Natali Prize in Human Rights Journalism, and the Vladimir Herzog Human Rights Award. Cavalcanti became well known in Brazil in 2012 when he was taken prisoner in Homs, Syria, despite having permission from the Assad government to travel there, and he was only released thanks to pressure from the Brazilian government.

NICK CAISTOR is an award-winning translator of more than fifty works from Spanish and Portuguese. He has also published short biographies of Octavio Paz, Fidel Castro, and Ernesto "Che" Guevara, as well as cultural histories of Buenos Aires and Mexico City.